A Musical
IN THE MAKING

Also by Mary O'Hara

MY FRIEND FLICKA

THUNDERHEAD

GREEN GRASS OF WYOMING

THE SON OF ADAM WYNGATE

NOVEL-IN-THE-MAKING

WYOMING SUMMER

THE CATCH COLT (A MUSICAL PLAY)

A Musical
IN THE MAKING

by Mary O'Hara

MARKANE PUBLISHING CO., INC.
Chevy Chase, Md.

Library of Congress Catalogue Card Number: 66-12949

Printed in the United States

MARKANE PUBLISHING CO., INC.
5506 Grove Street
Chevy Chase, Md.

A Musical
IN THE MAKING

One

I AM A CHILD, loving to write and tell stories, to compose music and play it on the piano and write it down in books of manuscript paper.

Someone said, These tunes of Mary's—why, they're like stage music. They could be the songs in a musical.

I was instantly certain. *When I'm grown up I'll write a musical.*

It became my dream; I did not doubt that it would go all the way to production and popularity. It took its place in my inner life and when I sat down at the piano to improvise, to play by ear, to compose, it emerged and hung there in the air, above and a little to the right—my mental eyes could see it complete with proscenium arch, curtain, footlights, and dancing figures.

I fell under its spell. I smiled at it.

Often I dreamed compositions. I kept a notebook and pencil beside my bed so that in the moment of waking I could jot them down before they fled.

I remember my misery when, once, I could not.

I had composed a quartet for piano, harp, and two violins, called the "Four Winds."

We were traveling in Europe, going from one Grand Hotel to the next: a family group of three generations including three children and two governesses of iron severity. There was simply no way in the world that I could make anyone see the necessity of procuring for me score paper suitable for having a quartet written upon it. There would be no use even in mentioning it. I would be told to pay attention to the lessons and practice hours that had been set me.

Of what a size, these European Grand Hotels! Whole armies could be lost in them. To an undersized little girl of eleven emerging, trembling, from her bedroom in the night, it seemed as if she were stepping out into a silent city where invisible thousands lay in rumpled beds, their mouths open, sleeping that deepest sleep of just before the dawn.

A governess sleeps in the same room with you. You could only escape if you slid out of bed and dressed yourself as silently as a shadow. The opening and closing of doors was difficult but there was a technique which must be mastered. She had mastered it, but Oh! that empty corridor! so wide, so long, stretching ahead like a city boulevard!

She clung to the walls, fearing creaks. Her slippered feet slid forward without a sound. She walked a long time before she reached the great open well of the broad stairway. Now her heart began to pound and came up in her throat. But because of her need to write the quartet she persisted, descending, clinging to the wall.

Below was the succession of common rooms: hall, reception rooms, lobby, lounge, tea room, smoking room, writing room—each one an empty chunk of space like a city plaza, and she had to leave the walls and strike out boldly. She glanced back with eyes of terror. . . .

Days ago, in the writing room, she had spotted the big thin white blotters on the desks.

Now she seated herself, drew out the ruler and sharp-pointed pencils she had brought with her, and fell into bliss. All fear left her. This was the familiar, heavenly trance of creation.

She wrote the score of the "Four Winds," folded the blotters as small as she could and thrust them inside the blouse of her frock.

She regained her room and slid under the bed-clothes.

In due time she was awakened by the governess and made ready for breakfast.

The manuscript was never discovered. It was tucked away in the small portfolio which each child was allowed to carry about Europe with her "private papers."

Children's daydreams—*Someday I'll*—are seldom taken seriously, even by themselves. Had I a real intention to write a musical or was it just an always-to-be dream? At any rate, since ours was a musical family, I went on with music as a mere matter of education. First our family elders taught us, then the governess, then professional teachers. I was taught my notes almost as soon as the alphabet.

There is that strange thing called "absolute pitch." It sounds as if it would mean so true an ear that the musician would never be off-pitch in singing, but it means something quite different: merely, that from birth on, the child knows the letter-name of whatever note he hears. A little three-year-old boy at kindergarten learning *do re mi fa sol la ti do* went into the yard at recess. A cockerel was strutting there. It crowed, *cock-a-doodle-doo!* and the child exclaimed, "He sang *La!*" The teacher ran in to the piano and touched A. The child had been right. He had absolute pitch.

This gift usually means great talent, but not always. Wagner had to do without it, also Leonard Bernstein and many other great musicians.

I did not have it, but did have good relative pitch, so that I always knew what note I was singing or whistling or thinking. It was this which enabled me to write down my compositions without going to the piano.

I learned music also by much hearing for I listened with intense concentration. We were taken to oratorios, to concerts at Carnegie Hall, to opera at the Metropolitan, to musical shows.

Our house was full of instruments. We picked them up and played them as we would learn to play a new game.

I grew up, married, moved away from my home in Brooklyn Heights to California.

I kept on with my two loves—writing and composing. Stories and articles, songs and dances, piano pieces. And I found that the artist's labor is endless. There are no hours, no holidays. Day and night the mind shuttles and weaves and the hand reaches for a pencil to jot down word-notes, music-notes.

I loved the labor, forgetting to eat, sleep, or rest. I wrote with passion.

Much of what I wrote was published. Hollywood drew me in and I made a name for myself as a scenario writer.

[4]

A music store in Los Angeles filled its windows with copies of a group of juvenile piano studies by me, and I stood in front of it, my face to the glass, looking and marveling. Could it be true?

I did not forget my dream.

I had a box with black-lettered label, "For The Musical." Into this went such compositions and themes as seemed to me suitable for the stage.

Someday, I would think, *Someday. . . .*

I moved from California to Wyoming and fell in love with emptiness and sky and wild horses and wrote my first full length novel, *My Friend Flicka,* then its sequel, then the sequel of the sequel. One by one they went on the screen, then into foreign translation, then on television.

The same Wyoming background would of course be the background for the musical. And now, familiar as I was with the western plains and the talk and doings of the people that lived there, I sketched a story for the play, I gave it a title *The Catch Colt,* and put it in the box.

I moved again. I heard myself say, "yes—back home again," meaning on the Atlantic coast where I had been born. This time, home was a roomy country house made out of an old Connecticut barn.

I had a music room which held my Mason and Hamlin grand piano, my tape recorder, T-V, Hi-Fi, and a whole cupboard of shelves with music and music books, including Grove's Dictionary of Music.

I had a writing room at the other end of the house equipped with tables for typewriters, shelves for manuscripts, and writing supplies.

My house was approached by a curving avenue of

[5]

trees between pastures on one side and woodland on the other. Sometimes, returning from the city I had seen deer bounding across the road in front of me to plunge into the cover of the forest.

The pastures were divided by old, grey stone walls.

The tall windows of my living room were filled with sky and clouds. At the back, they opened out onto a terrace twenty feet square with roof of wistaria and a view which sloped down and away across meadow and orchard to soft low hills, a dozen of them folding across each other and at last the misty horizon—all without a single habitation to be seen.

Driving out of the avenue on the other side of the house—really the front—I could reach the Merritt Parkway in twenty-five minutes; and from there to New York in an hour and a half.

Here I continued to write books and compose music and songs.

But not the musical. The musical was still just a dream.

It would require quite a shock to make me think of it as anything else.

Meanwhile, my life was passing.

The shock was administered one day in New York when I attended a luncheon given by the Father Keller Association to award the prizes in a four-year-old fiction, drama, and poetry contest.

Two

THE JUDGES sat at a long table on the dais. Members of the press filled the floor of the large hotel dining room.

I was one of the judges and beside me sat a well-known theatrical man.

"Why haven't you ever given us a musical, Miss O'Hara?" he asked, and there was no hesitation about my answer.

"Why, I'm writing a musical—I've been writing it for years!"

Before I had finished speaking he had gripped my hand. "I'll produce it!"

"Sight unseen?"

"Sight unseen if it has the western background of your Wyoming books."

Driving home on the Merritt Parkway that afternoon I thought over his words and smiled at his daring "Sight unseen." But not so daring, come to think of it, for from my books he could be sure I knew the Wyoming background—people, language, business. Also that I could create characters and build stories. If that much were handed him, even by a novice playwright, he, out of his experience, could shape it to the stage and put it on.

Not even the wheels under my car spun faster than my thoughts.

If I am ever going to do this musical, I told myself, I should do it now. I had no serious commitments. My son, Kent, was now an Air Force officer, living in Washington with his English wife and two little boys.

Since coming to Connecticut in 1948 I had worked incessantly; first, the re-modeling of my barn-house and writing of my big novel, published in 1952: *The Son of Adam Wyngate*. A year later, *Novel-in-the-Making*. Then two years work on music, principally an exhaustive revision of my piano "Étude" for which the publication contract had only recently been signed. So now decks were cleared for action. What action?

Miles passed.

Yes . . . if you don't do it now, you never will . . . because you don't really want it, you only want the dream . . .

That strange seduction of a dream; not only that it follows the slightest whim of its creator, as if a wand were waved, but a quality in itself that to me was pure charm, the quality of the far away and the never was: romance; illusion. Yes, a shimmering quality which softens and veils hard facts and adds luster and mystery.

But this illusion is inherent in the theatre. Its very self. When one sees that proscenium arch filled with the long folds of curtain—when one takes one's seat in the theatre, the spell falls upon one.

At that moment, I leave the real world behind and give myself to the enchantment. I await the thrilling moment when the curtain rises and a human figure moves out behind the footlights, and before my very eyes begins to live a life which is untrue and unreal—but so true and real that I have to believe it and clench my hands, hold my breath, smile, laugh—simply roar—with delight and amusement; or weep. In other words, a story! And the spell is the same spell that falls on a child when he opens a book and reads the words, *Once upon a time. . . .*

The vogue of today I knew to be realism rather than romance. But fiction can be both: romantic because it must have allure; realistic because it must have punch; the purely romantic is insipid; the purely realistic, drab.

Besides, I thought, everyone really loves romance.

There were certain other classifications to be considered. Musical comedy? Farce? Variety show? Revue? Light opera? Operetta?

But the playwright is not restricted; these can be used in any combinations he wishes. All are included in the general term, Musical Play.

Miles rolled under me. I passed Wilton, Westport, Easton, thinking hard. Was I ready?

For most of my life I had been practicing the dramatic arts. I had studied and read books of criticism, theatre notes, reviews in newspapers and periodicals; essays by columnists; biographies of actors, producers, choreographers, composers. I had listened to all such subjects being torn to tatters in endless arguments, and seen illustrated on the screen the harrowing business of getting a musical onto Broadway. This last entailed such outright suffering it reminded me of Hollywood and the teams of writers they sign up for weekly installments of radio serials; and the cold-blooded calculations in advance of just how long the writers will last before they

[9]

break down and are carried away on stretchers to the hospital while a new team is contracted for and brought in.

Opening night for a Broadway show was equally frightful. . . . authors, I have read, usually crouching in the men's room during the entire performance. . . . females fainting or "not being able to stop vomiting" —exhausted stagehands found lying in the aisles, faces up, in deep sleep-like coma.

I didn't doubt any of this. When Kent asked me if I thought I could stand it, I said, "I'll have nothing to do with it I'll create the play—music and book on paper. Then the producers can take over."

This was practically a vow.

I continued with my self-searching—did I really have all the necessary qualifications?

Are you sure you can write a good dramatic story? *Certainly I'm sure of that.* . . .

And versify? *As easily as talk.* . . .

Write good dialogue? *Always ready at the tip of my tongue.* . . .

Create appealing characters? *What about Ken and Flicka* . . . ?

Hit the popular taste? *Didn't they say in Hollywood, she has the common touch.* . . .

Then the music, what about your songs and dances? *Doesn't everyone gather around the piano and say play it again* . . . ?

As a single item in my list of qualifications the fact that I had the two natural gifts, writing and composing, outweighed all others.

It seems to be a classic combination, from Wagner down to our day with Gian-Carlo Menotti, Noel Coward, Meredith Wilson and many others. Anyone having the two gifts is almost certain to turn to the stage.

And think how much easier this is than a team of collaborators. I have heard that when they are putting on a musical, author and composer hardly dare be out of each others' sight.

Now you've got that, I told myself. You're lucky. Are you going to throw it away?

I took the ramp off the parkway and turned left, concluding that I was well prepared to write a musical —over prepared, if anything. There comes a time when preparing ought to stop. And doing begin.

Late afternoon traffic on the road coming up from Bridgeport slowed me down.

I was warning myself now. Expect one disappointment after the other. Don't expect quick results or, at first, any results at all.

I remembered the young California producer-actor who conceived the idea of getting from George Bernard Shaw (or his estate) stage-rights to *Pygmalion* for a Musical Play; while waiting for the deal to go through, he contracted Loewe & Lerner for music and book, then got a music publisher. While these powers and principalities were being collected, the producer unfortunately died; another producer stepped in; then Lerner and Loewe separated; then the stage rights were obtained; then a second music publisher outbid the first; then another composer and writer were engaged but could achieve nothing satisfactory; then Lerner and Loewe were united again and re-engaged. At this point, the infant project was at last standing on its own feet and taking a step or two forward. When *My Fair Lady* hit Broadway, nine years of work were behind it. To be in a state of hope and expectation for nine years, I told myself, might be very harrowing. And remember, in the end, it might never get off the ground. You're not George Bernard Shaw and Frederick Loewe and Alan Jay Lerner all combined . . .

But I would have had my fun. The years of happy working at my two specialities . . . and all the luck, good and bad . . . and the people—the new, interesting contacts.

I knew, too, that there were by-products, even for shows that failed on the stage. Screen rights, T.V., Radio. Possibly foreign stage rights.

Or I could make a "Symphonette" of the best of the music, and it might be performed for years. Many French composers had done that when an opera or operetta for which they had composed the music, failed as a stage show.

There would be many strings to my bow. All I had to do was begin it and see it through.

Moreover, don't get the idea you have to make a SMASH HIT.

I now outlined to myself just what it was I wanted to create.

Just an evening's pleasant, light entertainment. Three or four dollars worth. Something the whole family can see and enjoy.

It crossed my mind that this sort of thing was not exactly in style. Would anyone want it?

After some thought I answered that silly question. Of course they would. Everyone wants it.

Now a subtle excitement took possession of me. That was in 1955. It has never let go.

The excitement is made of tiny butterflies in the bloodstream, in every vein of the body, altering the pulse, making tensions, changing the look of the eye and all the rhythms and movements and steps and postures of the body.

I was driving too fast. Why start rushing now? You've got nine years to go. . . . I slowed up.

Turning into the Monroe Turnpike I told myself there was really not a single good reason—not one—why I should not do this.

But remember. *If you begin, it's going to take years —and you can't give up.*

This held me for six miles until I turned into my own driveway.

And really, if you don't do it now, you never will.

I eased the car across the service yard (being watchful of welcoming dogs, cats, and kittens) and into the subterranean garage, reviewing in my mind the various vague story lines I had sketched for the musical, selecting the salient points.

Before I took my hat off I went to the typewriter and wrote a brief sketch of the story. The next day I wrote another, two or three times as long. By the end of the week I had quite a full outline, and in a month a rough first draft of the play, including many lyrics.

Indeed I felt as if, coming up on the Merritt Parkway, I had begun, carried through, and completed the whole show.

Three

OPENING THE THEATRE section of the Sunday *New York Times* I became interested in an article dealing with the dearth of original stories for musicals. Aside from the ability to write them, it required, the columnist admitted, a good deal of courage. But it was difficult to believe that this ability and courage did not exist among our many authors and playwrights. Why, then, always adaptations of books or of plays, classical or modern, instead of originals?

I put the paper down, congratulating myself. *I* was writing an original for the musical stage.

I kept at the job. I was looking forward to the moment when my play would be in the hands of a producer. Before that happened I wanted all or nearly all the lyrics written and the story complete, if only in outline form. Besides that I wanted to have collected many critical opinions about the show.

Every author loves his own brain children, but others must love them too if there is to be a success. Others by the millions.

I must find out how others felt about 1) the background, the Wyoming ranch, which was folksy Americana; 2) the title, *The Catch Colt;* 3) the subject, a lost boy; 4) the theme, when you get what you want you don't want it; 5) the plot, which was, really, just the classical old fable: penniless adventurer falls in love with king's daughter and she with him; to get rid of him, he is set a nearly impossible task but when, with her help, he succeeds, he then must kill an ogre before he can win the princess.

Opinions, however, unless delivered by an expert can be dangerous. Ask an opinion of a member of the family, or casual friends or acquaintances, and what you will get may be something they have recently heard someone else say, or it may mirror some personal dislike or prejudice, or you may be asking someone who habitually sees defects rather than virtues, or who likes to criticize, or who follows always the most conventional formulae.

If you are asking an expert, the opinion will be worth its weight in gold. They will point out the strength as well as the weakness, the fresh and original as well as the trite, show you where danger lies; or give you the stimulating lift that puts fresh heart into you.

But there are not many experts. And it is hard to get to them. So much the better thing is not to ask people for opinions, but manoeuvre to get an emotional reaction from them. There is all the difference in the world between an opinion and a reaction and it is a real tragedy that this distinction is not better understood. The distinction is that between thinking and feeling.

Don't trouble to find out what a person thinks about your piece, find out how it makes him feel. Display it to him. Tell the story, wordpaint the scenes, and watch his

[15]

face. If he is bored his attention will be perfunctory or non-existent. If he has agreed to listen to you or invited your performance, he is in politeness bound to give at least some admiration and approval and suppress his doubts, and you must be on the lookout for this and discount it.

But if you are holding him, his eyes will widen, the expression around his mouth change, the lips shape themselves into exclamations; or there will be the sudden laugh or sparkle in the eye, or the delighted scream of surprise; or he may interrupt with a question which will be valuable for you. "I didn't get that" . . . "What was it she said?" And so on.

The thing that makes or breaks a piece is the emotion it does or does not kindle.

So I talked about my show, first to my good friends, Charles and Kay. As soon as I had a fairly complete script I read it to them.

The story had not changed much from the outline I wrote when I was living in Wyoming. There was still the Harvard professor, ex-professor, old and discredited, who had gone to Wyoming to hunt for the lost grandson. There was still the twenty-year-old ranch hand who didn't know who he was, a 'catch colt' who came to the ranch looking for a job on the hay crew. When he wanted to marry Letty, the daughter of the boss, he was told by Letty's mother "Not good enough for *my* daughter—not good enough for any woman's daughter."

And tell the audience right at the start without trying to build up surprise, that the old sheepherder, looking for a lost grandson, is the professor, and the 'catch colt' is the grandson. The play will be about the de-

[16]

ciphering of the mystery and getting actual proof of the relationship.

As far as I could tell, Charles and Kay were held to the very end. It was really a hilarious evening. There was far more humor than I had counted on, even allowing for their friendly prejudice in my favor.

Charles said, "I've been to a show and enjoyed every scene and every word of it—all without leaving my own house. More entertaining than many a show I've seen at the Schubert."

Then I let all my friends know about it and found that, here in Monroe, it added quite a spice to the general conversation.

At one Sunday afternoon party when a score of Marian's friends were assembled on the stone-floored patio of her old New England farmhouse, she urged me to ". . . tell us all about it! . . . Listen, everybody! Mary's going to tell us the story of her musical!"

It was a good chance, I saw, for an audition. So I did it, and did the best I could by it, interrupted many a time by laughs and exclamations. When it was over there was an outburst of enthusiasm. Congratulations. Also warnings.

"Oh my! You don't know what you're getting into! Try-outs in Philadelphia and Boston and New Haven! Endless rehearsing and re-writing. . . ."

"Yes! Working all night—sleeping all day. . . ."

"Traveling with a theatrical company. . . ."

"Everybody hugging and kissing. . . ."

One man said, "I have a friend who is a producer. He likes this sort of thing—Americana, isn't it? I'll tell him about it."

Another said, "When the time comes, I'll put you in touch with the man who finances most of the Broadway shows—I went to school with him."

Books were sent to me. One was a best-seller called *Say Darling!,* most amusing, about a man who had sold the stage rights of his recently published novel and was asked to go to New York and help make a musical of it.

The other was a running diary or "log" written by a playwright who was working on his play along with the producers. This one was more serious, giving dates and figures, facts, delays of years, incomprehensible disappointments, double-crossings. Both ended, of course, with the usual SMASH HIT.

Most of what I read cheered me about my play and warned me against having anything to do with the production—never, never, never.

Old Mrs. Shepard, about ninety and bed-ridden, read the script and commented shrewdly, "This Joey must be some punkins to *do* all that, *be* all that, *sing* all that." This, suggesting that the female star was put into the shade by the male, worried me a little.

Occasionally, I am asked to lecture on fiction-writing to groups of students, or at clubs or colleges.

At this time I was scheduled to give such a lecture at the Cosmopolitan Club in New York, and at the end of my talk, there was the usual short session of informal questions-and-answers.

One woman put up her hand. "Is it true, Miss O'Hara, that you're writing a musical? We heard you were."

I admitted it was true.

"What's it about?"

I was glad I could answer with something brief and striking. "A lost boy."

There were excited exclamations, approving laughter; a hand shot up and waved violently. "I'll come," she screamed. "I've always wanted to know what became of them!"

My memory leaps forward several years here, to a day when I sat at luncheon in a little restaurant in Paris and was asked the same question, "What's it about?" by my French publisher. I made the same answer, watching his handsome saturnine face.

The smile deepened as he said, "And of course he turns out to be the prince and marries the princess."

I assented. He suggested, "Why not put it on here in Paris? Our productions are famous."

Kent, who was with me, said, "What I want her to do is make a book out of it first. I tell her that's the golden key to a Broadway show."

The publisher beamed. "And I will publish it."

And in this manner, fishing for reactions, I did find out that there was what appeared to be irreconcilable differences of opinion on two points; first, the title; second, the lead. Should it be the boy's story or the old man's. Some claimed that to make the boy the lead would mean a musical that was just another boy-meets-girl story—very trite. But if the lead was Windy that would really be something original and different. The professor who became a sheepherder had turned out to be a very sympathetic character. People fell in love with him. He was surely a bit balmy, going around always asking "Has anyone seen my little boy?" But that turn of the head, that far searching look in the eye—somehow it was moving.

The question had to be decided at the very beginning and I had decided it. Youth is far more attractive than age. Youth is more popular. No one seeks out the old, or enjoys them, or wants to be old themselves or, if they are, to have their age noticed or noticeable. The whole world pursues youth and loves it. And this holds for stage and screen as well as life. An aged character on stage, if pathetic, is repellent. One must turn one's eyes away. Only if comic, outrageous, or grotesque (like Ethel Barrymore's portrayal of Gran) can it be enjoyed.

And this, really, it would break my heart to do. Let the young be comic and grotesque if they want (and many of them do want) but let age put on its mask of unconcern and dignity and hide its defeats.

The other point on which there was disagreement was the title.

Titles are always difficult.

Many a show gets to Broadway miscalled—only later to find its right name. As *On The Town* was first called *Fancy Free. My Sister Eileen* became *Wonderful Town. Oklahoma!* was first, *Away We Go!*

For my show I had considered *The Man from Windy River* as well as *The Catch Colt.*

Quite by accident I annexed a new title at the cocktail party given for authors by the Dramatists Guild in New York at which reporters and interviewers and critics were invited to meet authors.

Asked by a newspaper columnist, "What are you doing now, Miss O'Hara?" I said I was writing a musical.

"Oh, you don't say! And what's the title? What's the locale?"

Answering the last of the two questions with a lackadaisical wave of the hand, I said modestly, "Oh—Wyoming!"

"*Oh! Wyoming!*" she exclaimed, "What's a title! Genius, Miss O'Hara, Genius!"

Thus by chance this title was handed me and set me thinking. Perhaps the best yet, I thought. After all, the western term "catch colt" had to be explained. Joey, in the show, explains it, singing "wandering strays they are and I'm the same—no father, no mother, not even a real last name." Unexplained, it is puzzling, which is usually a drawback.

On the other hand, visualizing it in lights over a theatre it looked striking. Short, strong, strange. And that no one would know what it meant might add rather than detract. I remembered the Broadway hit *The Shrike.* No one understood that either. People talked about it, explaining. An effective title, I thought.

As for *Oh! Wyoming!* Suppose people thought it was copied from *Oklahoma!*? This, however, seemed a far-fetched idea. Surely there could be a musical for every state in the union—how stunning that would be! And the name of the state should be in every title and if there was an Oh before it, what matter? Before I was through with this title I was to find out how much it mattered. Meanwhile, I continued trying it out.

Talking to the young doctor who put the hypodermic needle into my arm, the magic fortnightly shot which keeps me from ever, ever having a cold:

[21]

"Which title would you prefer. *The Catch Colt?* or *The Man from Windy River?* or *Top of the Big Hill?* or *Oh! Wyoming!?* Think it over and tell me next time I come."

"I don't need to think it over," said the young man rubbing alcohol violently on my arm. "I can tell you now. *The Catch Colt.*"

"But why?"

"Oh, because it's new and different. We've had the man from this and the man from that. But a *Catch Colt* —what the heck is it, anyway? Nobody knows. That's *something*. It's intriguing!"

But someone else said, "Why, Mary, *Oh! Wyoming!* is the title. There's no comparison. If I was an out-of-town man and went to New York and wanted to go to a show and looked over the titles, that title *Oh! Wyoming!* would get me in! And Mary—tell you something—it's the Oh! does it!"

In time I arrived for cocktails in the New York apartment of Jean Dalrymple.

Hers is a big name in the New York theatre. She is the directress of the City Center Light Opera Company and also the link with the Ford Foundation which puts up a lot of the money.

It is generally understood that they wish to encourage Americana, so this was an important meeting which had been brought about by a personal letter from a mutual friend to General Ginder, Jean's husband.

A few of her friends were present, and the mood of the little gathering, with the late afternoon cocktails, was so gay, so optimistic, that it was hard to get down to any sort of business.

When we did, she was surprised to find out that the play was not an adaptation of one of my books.

"An original?" she exclaimed.

"Yes."

Her eyebrows went up.

"Isn't everybody looking for originals?" I asked.

"I should say not!"

"But why not?"

There was now quite a lengthy discussion of originals. The risk taken by any producer and the difficulties he invited if he was foolhardy enough to put on an original musical. Nothing was tried and true; nothing was certain, not even the fact that it had merit enough to be put on at all. Even if it had, it was not yet crystallized: lines, business, action, even certain turns and twists of the plot could be either this way or that; and such things were only really decided and settled for good and all by use—and time. Like the Gilbert and Sullivan operettas; or the HIT modern musicals; like *The King and I;* or Molnar's plays—*Carousel* or *The Merry Widow;* or the operettas of Gian-Carlo Menotti. All these have been successfully produced so often that all the questions have been answered. All a producer had to do was copy and do it well.

Moreover, the music had all been recorded. The actors could buy the records and learn their songs by ear, instead of being given pages of brand new music, never performed or even heard before, to be read and studied and learned.

"And if, in addition, it is not an adaptation of a well known book but an entirely new story. . . ."

I told her of the article I had read in the *Times,*

[23]

urging playwrights to write directly for the musical stage.

"Just some columnist's theory," she answered. "Producers want to play safe. And you can't blame them. It costs a fortune to put a show on."

Considerably deflated, I pointed out that when a publisher publishes a book by an unknown author—as they often do—they are taking the same sort of risk.

She answered, "Of course. Moreover, if no producer was ever willing to take the gamble, we'd never have any new shows. So, here at City Center, though our rule is only to put on revivals, we do sometimes produce an original." She beamed and I was able to breathe again. "We pride ourselves on it."

"How often?" I asked.

"As a matter of fact, very seldom. They have to be outstanding."

She then asked me to tell her my story. She listened attentively, and it revived me a little to see that it was making its usual good impression. I answered innumerable questions and began to hope it might prove to be that outstanding exception.

"And what title?" she asked.

"How would you like, *The Catch Colt?*"

"Catch cold!" She made a face. "God forbid!"

"Then how would you like *Oh! Wyoming?*"

She rose swiftly to her feet. She is a little thing, pretty and blond, and was dressed in a low-necked pink frock. She had formerly been an actress.

"Excellent! A commercial title!"

We were drinking champagne cocktails. She lifted

[24]

her glass from the table and held it high, looking at the amber fluid.

Then she smiled at me, smiled around the room and spoke the astonishing words. "I like the story. I like the title. I'll produce it! Here's to *Oh! Wyoming!*"

I walked away, pleased and exhilarated, but somehow without too much confidence in a City Center production. Her last words had been that she would take it up with her committee immediately (I gathered these were members of the Ford Foundation) and let me know.

I expected word from her almost daily but no word came.

If she was going to refuse, I told myself, she would return the script. But no script came.

Months passed. I wrote her—no answer. Then, at last, I telephoned and we talked. It began with apologies on her part. No—the committee had turned the show down, for the present; perhaps if I could get a production elsewhere first, City Center might make it as a revival— that was their usual procedure; might she keep the script? She really did like the play and would bear it in mind. Meanwhile, if we put out any publicity or interested a producer, we had her permission to use her name as someone interested. . . .

I felt definitely encouraged. Remember, I told myself, nine years. . . . this was only the start.

I talked about a City Center production to everyone who I thought might know anything about it. I learned that their orchestra of forty pieces was magnificent. The theatre was splendid. A musical put on there would really be in a show case for Broadway producers to see. If it was successful, it could be taken from there to Broadway where it could have a run of indefinite length. In any case it would be an honor and distinction to be produced there and would mean that an original had made good.

Meanwhile, there was much to do. Endless work in music room and writing room. Endless happy hours, actually the happiest of my life, for never before had I made my principle occupation this fusing of music and story.

Four

A STORY EVOLVES. What at first seems good is presently surpassed by something else, or is thrown into an unfavorable light and must be changed. Make one change and, usually, you have to make a dozen. Your desk, your room becomes littered with rewritten scenes and sheets of dialogue.

Those terrible hours, or even days or weeks, when a writer is "stuck" are fearful experiences, as every writer knows. There seems absolutely nothing that is just right and yet the story is not told. I believe it would be possible, sitting there at the typewriter waiting and tensely concentrated, to lose consciousness.

So take what comes whenever it comes, even though it is not in chronological sequence; an abundance of material is invaluable; and if this means overwriting at first, still no harm is done—it can always be cut.

I was overwriting extravagantly. Get everything on paper—dialogue, lyrics, much business, movement, and action.

Some of this was written out in meticulous detail as it would appear on the stage—every glance, gesture, word. Some was in outline. All together it made smooth reading.

I arranged cartons labeled Discards from Version One, Discards from Version Two, Discards from Version Three, etc.

Over and over again I went back to the fundamental analysis. My musical was a *fantasy,* firstly because all musicals are (so says Eric Bentley) and secondly because it had a scene of outright magic at the end of the first act. As follows: my hero, the dreamy boy, the singer of songs, lover of the sweet smell of hay, was commanded to perform a mechanical job which had stumped all the men on the ranch—erect a modern windmill out of a Sears Roebuck package of parts. The penalty of failure: "get off the ranch." All so impossible for Joey that, after one or two futile attempts (about the middle of the first act), he drops his tools, turns away, and begins to sing charming songs about Letty. Letty interrupts him, urging him to do the job; he explains that he can think of nothing but her, and if she would only give him some encouragement (holding out his arms to her) it would make a superman of him and he could do anything. When, after a good deal of singing back and forth, she goes into his arms, the windmill, miraculously, rises from the pile of parts.

Pure magic, of course, and I had some qualms about it. Would the public accept it? But *Peter Pan* arranged as a musical was running on Broadway, a smash hit, nothing but magic from beginning to end. *Carousel* had an entire second act made of magic. There were other plays with totally unreal dream sequences. Besides, if not a physical truth, there was a moral and metaphysical truth here— love can accomplish anything.

[28]

My concern was on the score of consistency. There was nothing else in the least magical in the play and I did not want there to be. Would the audience be impatient with Joey's subsequent troubles, always expecting him to pull more rabbits out of hats? I hoped not. I wanted all that followed of suspense and threat to be real and factual. But I wanted the magic windmill too. The sight of it rising suddenly into the air was too theatrical, too dramatic to lose. I kept it.

This was only one of the close decisions I had to make. It proved to be right.

There was also the question as to how long the speeches of the characters should be. This was a poser, for you can say the same thing in a hundred words, or fifty, or ten, or three.

For instance, Joey's remark when he comes asking for a job on the hay crew: "Late fer hayin', ain't it?" was first answered by Jim, the buckhouse cook, in forty words. "The boss bin waitin' fer rain—one good rain woulda put another foot on the red-top and hundreds o' bucks in his pocket—but no rain! And the grass jess burnin' up—hardly any water left in the ditches."

I could have made it, "Bin waitin' fer rain."

Which should it be?

I sought the answer by going to see the musicals that were runnning on Broadway. I was astounded by the amount of talk, so much of it unnecessary. The actors rattled it very fast with an overlap to the answering speech. I disliked this. It gave a hurried, forced, and artificial effect that was disturbing. Besides, it made the sentence difficult to understand. Would not a few words, more slowly and naturally articulated, have made a better impact on the audience? Supposing, in all that fast talk you missed something essential? Then you lost the story line and might never catch on again, drift along, missing everything.

My personal preference is for rather short, crisp dialogue. This is not very realistic, for in real life people are terribly long-winded and rather incoherent. But in my books I wanted to be considerate of my reader and limited myself to paragraphs of no more than moderate length. I thought that for a play they ought to be shorter still.

I managed to get a look at the manuscripts of several musicals and again was astounded. Some paragraphs of talk ran for half or three quarters of a page, some over a page. What a feat of memorizing for the actor!

I was reluctant to be convinced of the wisdom of this, but some reading I did at that time, memoirs of a famous Broadway director, confirmed it. He said to the author, "Words! Words! Give me more words! There are never enough words!" And in the autobiography of an operatic composer was the statement; "I always had to send the libretto back to the author asking for more words."

So I made my decision—and made it wrong. Eventually, I was to cut the dialogue to the bone.

The more Broadway shows I saw the more I was convinced that the lack of story interest was the reason many failed.

The reviews were monotonous. "No story" or "A weak book—as usual". One musical out of every ten that reach Broadway makes a hit and a fortune. Two out of five break even, three out of five are total failures. And yet, with one of these story-less scripts, producers are willing to go into production, angels are willing to invest up to half a million dollars.

What gives them this confidence? They seem to believe that by magnificent sets and costumes, or swinging and circling stages, or choreographic novelties, they can command and fascinate an audience.

Or possibly they put their faith entirely in the actors. An outstanding performance by a single actor or actress *could* put over and carry a show, even without a good story. But I shuddered at the thought of depending on such a *tour de force*. It might come off. But oh, it might not, it might not! And it is when you have staked all on something like that—so chancey—that it does not come off.

In Hollywood I had seen many a production planned with nothing more than an idea to start with.

An idea—with a certain background, certain star, and a million dollars to swing it. The whole studio gets hepped up. Scenarists, dialogue writers are engaged. Publicity begins to pour. Then it hesitates, stalls. New writers are engaged. But it won't go. It marks time, finally dissolves into waste and nothingness because the IDEA would not turn into a real story.

Everybody knows all this, I told myself, so why do they disregard it? They must have noticed that people are entertained merely by hearing a story *told*. Tell stories to children—they won't let you stop. Stories can be told on the stage without any trimmings or sets or mountings at all, the way the Chinese do, and still hold an audience.

A book publisher was talking to me one day about the number of failures they had. He was very disgrun-

[31]

tled. His plaint was that publishers, after the most careful calculations, bought and published works of fiction and launched them with expensive publicity, only to have them rejected by the public and returned in streams from the bookshops. When I replied, Why on earth don't you select better stories? I drew down upon my head an exceedingly long dissertation, all to the effect that no one, but NO ONE, could tell in advance whether it was a good story or not.

Perhaps this is the worst thing writers have to face. On paper, good stories so often go unrecognized.

But good books *are* published. Good musicals *are* made. Someone has recognized them when they were just on paper. Who?

Book publishers employ readers, mostly young women just out of college, and now and then a seasoned critic of distinction. They read, appraise, condemn or recommend.

Theatrical producers are apt to delegate the reading to some member of their family, wife or teen-age daughter—or to a secretary or switch-board operator.

One can hardly blame them for not reading scripts themselves. It is awfully hard work. It is just terrible. Asked to read a script, you are certain in advance that it is no good, that it is just another fizzle like all the others. Unless you have the eager hope of finding something good—more than hope, *belief* that there is a veritable jewel hidden in those pages, you can hardly bear to undertake the task, let alone put your mind honestly and deeply on it, reading it all through from start to finish.

Of all of this I had intimate personal experience, for my first work for the Hollywood studios was as a reader. My job was to find stories for the studio to make movies from. The crying need of every studio was for stories. They never had enough. I was to read all, *all* the fiction that was in submitted scenarios or books and magazines; write thumbnail sketches of them, and recommend or reject.

I was crazy about the job and could not feel that it would be at all difficult. I have always been a reader and I read fast. Surely story material was pouring out of the creative American mind by the millions of words. I would read those millions of words and find many stories.

I inquired about the reader who had preceded me on this job and was told she had been a distinguished Englishwoman, an Oxford graduate; she had really been wonderful, her little synopses and criticisms so scholarly, so polished—gem-like little essays. . . .

"And how many stories did she find for you in the year?"

She had not found any.

This, to me, meant that she had not recognized any. Good dramatic material *must* have passed through her hands. She had doubtless criticized them with her mind only, not noticing whether there was anything that gripped her, made her turn the pages faster, made her tense and expectant.

I thought it was pretty hard luck for the author. And also for the studio.

I took my work seriously. I found that good stories were rare. I found, too, that recognition was not so easy. I sometimes sat with the story in my hands, weighing it. Yes?—or no? I found, to my horror, that certain things quite unrelated to the story were influencing me. What time was it? Nearly time to go home? I had been reading for six hours and tended to drop whatever was in my hands into the discard basket and reach for my hat and coat. Or I had already found one story that afternoon and had, in jubilation, telephoned the office of the director who was frantic for a vehicle for his star. It would be most unlikely that there would be another story on the same day; why, actually, they did not come along even once a month.

But I did find stories, recognized them, recommended them; and they were made into pictures. Eleven in that year. One afternoon I found three in a row. So I knew that whatever the faculty of recognition is, I had it.

I have often wondered what is behind it. Possibly one must have retained that child-like ability to be moved. In spite of the fact that my work, my whole life, was spent in the most professional and sophisticated surroundings, and that by now I might be expected to be *blasé* and bored, I was not. I could still quite easily fall victim to the spell, and find my mouth open in wonder as I turned the pages. When this happened I knew that somewhere in those pages, even though hidden by bad writing and weak construction, lay story situations worth developing and putting on the screen.

There was constant pressure on me. Once, a "big" director was needing a story. He was idling, waiting, drawing his terrific salary week by week, kicking a football out in the lot with one of the prop boys, or playing with the wet clay in one of the sculptor's studios; and the executives of the studio, nearly out of their minds, were bringing stuff in arm-loads to my office for me to read.

At about three one afternoon, a book was brought me with the information that (hopefully) this might be it.

It was just out, by an important author, and the New York office had taken an option on it that would expire at midnight tonight. Another studio was trying to get it.

The director would not interrupt his football until he had a synopsis from me. Could I read it and write the *précis* immediately—and fast.

"Well—it won't be done by closing time."

"We'll stay open."

In an hour I sent word to the director, "This is your next picture." He came to my office, wanting the synopsis, sitting down to wait for it. Executives crowded at my door. Telephone lines to the New York office were humming.

I asked to be alone while I worked.

At five-thirty, closing time, the studio emptied and went dark; all except the writers' wing. Two typists were held, half a dozen of us remained.

Coffee and sandwiches were sent over from the "quick and dirty" across the street.

The option was taken up before midnight and Rex Ingram made *Scaramouche*.

Five

So THE STORY'S the thing.

It has to be written, offered, read, recognized, and bought.

When I became a free-lance scenario writer I decided that what I had often said in jest was actually true. Producers can't read.

But why should it be expected of them? To be able to read, in the sense of reading, comprehending, and judging, is a specialty. So is it a specialty to be able to sign big checks. Perhaps they don't go together.

A writer, newly engaged, may meet the head of the studio once or twice, but their association is slight. The writer's office is in the story department and his immediate supervisor is the story editor. The fabulous offices of the top executive, usually referred to as the Big Boy, are in the upper regions.

Who is it then, who is going to convey what is in the writer's mind skyward to where the checks are signed? It may be the story editor, or possibly a certain director or star, or some liaison officer engaged just for the purpose of linking the upper and lower echelons.

I had, by now, acquired something of a name as free

lance writer and was once sent for to undertake the scen-
arizing of a popular novel for one of the studios. I liked
the story. It had a charming theme: young man falls in
love with a ghost. The appointment for an interview was
with Mr. Brisbane, a recently acquired story editor—a
distinguished literary man from New York with whom I
was acquainted.

All this seemed very promising.

Having arrived at the studio, I found that Mr. Brisbane could not be seen until after lunch. Would I please
have luncheon with Mrs. Tuttle? She knew all about the
story and the way it was to be treated. In fact, she was on
the production staff. Mr. Brisbane would be back after
lunch and we could have our interview then.

We lunched in the big studio restaurant. Mrs. Tuttle pointed out the stars, many of them of course in cos-
tume and make-up, and gave me tid-bits of studio gossip.

Finally we got chatting about the story and I gathered that Mrs. Tuttle was one of these liaison officers who
operated between the story department and executive
offices above.

She had, she confessed, the ability so to tell a story,
half acting it as she talked, that she could get it over without reference to script or book—certainly a god-send to a
busy executive.

Now about this story—she had some ideas which he
liked. In fact, she had invented a complete "treatment,"
and *he* was sold on it.

The basic idea of the book—all that ghost part—
was, of course, ridiculous and would be thrown away.

As we arrived at dessert I saw that I was facing a very
different situation from what I had anticipated.

[37]

When we left the table she suggested that I come to her office before seeing Mr. Brisbane and read the "treatment?" It wasn't long. And she could explain it to me just as she had explained it to *him*. She thrust out her closed fist with the thumb pointing straight up. "The Big Boy has O.K.'d it, you know."

So I went to her office and read the treatment while she walked about nervously, talking in low tones to her secretary and fussing with the papers on her desk.

I finished it and laid it down, saying politely, "I'm afraid I couldn't do it." I got to my feet.

She darted about like a distracted bird. "Oh, but you simply don't get it, Miss O'Hara. Let me explain." And she began to act and to illustrate.

I sat down again and gave her my complete attention, listening intently, watching closely. She worked very hard, occasionally casting frantic glances at my face.

"That storm, for instance," she exclaimed, hurling herself about the office as the great waves might have hurled her "such a storm as never was—they both almost drown. . . ."

The storm went on for some time while I was thinking that, by now, Hollywood must have all its great spectacles on tape; storms, avalanches, train-wrecks, etc., filed away as stock shots, ready to be taken out and used any time, or sold by the yard if occasion offered. Big spectacles are always convenient when story values are lacking.

At last Mrs. Tuttle rose out of the waves, wiping tears, saliva, and foam from her face, and came to the scene in the garage where the assembled mechanics had paused from their labor to discuss Communism.

"But there wasn't any garage in the book," I objected. "Or Communists."

"Of course not. This will be instead of all that other stuff about the ghost."

"And in the book, the girl wasn't crazy." I objected further, getting to my feet. "I'm sorry, Mrs. Tuttle, but I couldn't do it. I really couldn't."

"But why? Why?"

"Well—all those disconnected elements—how do you expect them ever to hang together?"

She bowed charmingly. "That will be for you to do, Miss O'Hara! That will be *your* work! That is why you are here, and we know you can do it."

I couldn't help laughing a little. "Perhaps someone else can, but to me it just doesn't seem possible. There's really no use in my seeing Mr. Brisbane."

In distress, she clutched my arm. "But you can't possibly tell so soon, Miss O'Hara, you haven't even *tried*. Won't you even *try*?"

I considered, casting my mental eye again through the story. Was there any angle which would draw all these diverse (and, to me, crazy) ideas into significant relation with each other? I kept shaking my head.

"I can always tell at first reading whether the story will fall apart or hold together. Honestly, I couldn't do this, Mrs. Tuttle—I'm sorry."

(I've always been a firm believer in running away from trouble, even when it's far in the future.) She saw I was gathering my things, edging toward the door. . . .

She rushed to the telephone and called Brisbane.

Politely I waited, going to the small wall mirror and taking my compact out of my handbag.

She put down the telephone and turned to me, beaming. "Mr. Brisbane's in his office and he's very eager to see you."

I closed my purse and smiled. "I'll be glad to see him again," I said, and took leave of her.

Mr. Brisbane seemed a bit sulky as we exchanged greetings. I did not think it worth while to sit down, but stood, explaining how sorry I was—just not my sort of a job.

"But I do think you could give it a try, Miss O'Hara. One doesn't expect to pull off a good picture without a lot of hard work. This novel was a best-seller, you know, a big hit all over the country."

"Of course," I agreed, "I loved it too—but not these garage mechanics, these Communists, this crazy girl. Why, Mr. Brisbane, I *couldn't*. Really it isn't possible. Not for me, anyway. But if you want to go back to the original book—that would be different."

He gave a small helpless shrug of his shoulders.

"You're probably right," he said in the same sulky way, "but there's nothing I can do. This is the story as it's going to be shot." We looked at each other. He lifted his right fist with the thumb pointing up. I laughed and nodded and we said good-by.

In the hall, as I hurried, with a sense of escape, toward the elevator, a tall, handsome young man overtook me.

"Miss O'Hara, isn't it? I'm Turnbull, Jim Turnbull. I'm the director of this production you know. I've just heard you've turned us down. I'm sorry for that, Miss O'Hara. Won't you come to my office and talk it over?"

Then there was another fifteen minutes of being politely regretful, explaining that it just wasn't my sort of story.

"What is your principle reason for refusing, Miss O'Hara?"

[40]

During all of these interviews I was very careful of all that I said. I explained now that it was my policy never to undertake a script unless I had complete confidence in the story. "Otherwise I couldn't do my best work, it wouldn't really be fair to the studio."

"And you have not confidence in this?"

"That's it." Again the polite good-bys, and he walked down the corridor with me. His parting words were charming. "This makes me all the more anxious to work with you on a story in which you *do* have confidence."

I beamed at him. "I would like that very much too."

We shook hands, and he put me in the elevator.

At a certain point I always have the impulse to stop being diplomatic, just to blurt out the truth.

You had a good story! You bought it! Paid good money for it! The whole country had been charmed with it! Just try talking about ghosts one evening after dinner when a group of friends are gathered around the fire—they won't stop! At midnight they'll still be yarning and make-believe shuddering and looking over their shoulders into the dark corners, and saying "Hush! Did you hear that?" You had it! And threw it away for a mixture that wouldn't even make good hash!

Recognition again—or the lack of it. Some person must have recognized it, the New York reader probably. It was bought, then thrown away.

But not even this experience and others like it, took away all my hope of someday selling an original to one of the studios. They were in as great need of story material as ever, and producers kept deploring (in newspaper articles) the lack of originals for the screen.

So I kept writing originals, quite a number of them, and submitting them. And never sold one.

One of these was *My Friend Flicka* in short story form of about five thousand words.

I submitted it through a story department whose editor I knew personally.

He told me it was a good little story, but the studio's policy was, now, to produce only plays that had actually reached the Broadway stage, or books that had been published and made the best-seller list.

He suggested, with a great big grin, "All you have to do is make a full-length novel of it. Take it to New York. Get it published. Get it on the best-seller list!" We both laughed.

But unbelievably and inconceivably, that is just what happened.

I embarked on a freighter that was going from San Diego through Panama to New York, and the tale of my journey could be made into a story itself; entitled *The Price She Paid.*

There was a terrible storm.

I was sick all the time; most of the crew were sick.

The little old shriveled French captain called it a pretty dirty blow.

We ploughed and rolled and pitched our way down the coast of California and Mexico.

A great wave carried a man overboard. Bells clanged, the engines reversed, the ship halted and bucked. Another wave hurled the man back onto the deck and he clung to the hatch.

The Captain sustained and comforted me. He made me sit at table with him and eat potatoes. He squeezed

lemons for me, saying, It is better—if you can. . . . if
you can. . . .

When the rain stopped he made me go on deck and
held me firmly against the rail, his little thin arm, like
iron, around me. And while I, in company with all that I
could see of waters and waves and skies, swirled and
swayed and sagged, he told me tales of sea-faring to dis-
tract my mind. ". . . . the worst—the very worst that
ever happened to me was right in this place here, off
Chapultapec. Not a storm that time, but a fog, so thick it
was like blankets wrapped around us. I was here at the
rail like this and there was a sound like two pieces of silk
rubbed together, and suddenly I was looking at another
face leaning over another rail, not two yards away . . .
another ship there. I could have touched that face with its
wide open mouth . . . all the teeth showing . . . eyes
rolling . . . like a Gargoyle . . . not horrible really
but looking so because of his terror . . . and then it was
gone and there was nothing but the fog . . . gone just
like that! (The captain snapped his fingers) I never knew
what the ship was . . ."

The skies cleared and it was a pale twilight.

After dinner we walked the deck.

He was telling me now about the singing of Nelson
Eddy. How, when he listened, his hair stirred on his
head, and he lifted off his cap and drew up between his
fingers a little scalplock of hair.

The moon came out, a thin feather of a new moon
with a star, very small and pale almost within the
horns.

The captain replaced his cap and we both looked at
the moon.

"What makes it so beautiful?" he asked, musing. "I think it is the star, don't you? Yes, it is the star."

"Yes, it is the star," I echoed.

And as all the links of a chain have to do with each other, no matter how distant, so all this had to do with the musical—getting *My Friend Flicka* to market by means of the voyage: the captain, the man overboard, the collision, the Gargoyle, the potatoes, the lemons, the moon and the star, and the hair rising on his head when Nelson Eddy sings.

As with the old woman who at first complained that stick wouldn't beat dog, dog wouldn't bite pig, piggie wouldn't get over the stile and so she couldn't get home that night and then rejoiced that fire began to burn stick, stick began to beat dog, dog began to bite pig, piggie got over the stile and so she got home that night—just so I rejoiced. For—the story fell into the hands of one of those recognizers. And became a novel; the novel was published; the book went on the best-seller list; moved up to head place; was bought for the movies; went onto the screen; into European translations; into South American, into Asian translations; onto television.

When I had first offered it, in a short story, to a studio, it could have been bought for five thousand dollars, or even less.

In the final event, when the pig had got over the stile, the amount of the purchase price was headlined in the Los Angeles newspapers as $45,000.

Six

MY DREAM MUSICAL had, by now, acquired quite a little substance. Many people knew about it. It entered into conversations. Newspapers had written about it.

I began work every morning, according to my custom, before the sun rose, and continued until I was so tired I could work no more.

A revised script of the play had gone to a typing bureau and I had half a dozen clean copies.

Kent was vitally interested in it. We talked about it over the long distance telephone.

When winter came I rented a furnished house in Washington near him and made the trip down there and back quite often. Occasionally something, perhaps an indispensable reference book or some pages of manuscript (once it was my cat), got lost, and I had to drive back and forth.

The wheels under me, as usual, did their good work for me, freeing my mind in some peculiar fashion to examine every detail of the show. I covered the miles at the exact posted speed limit. I did not exceed. I had been arrested too often.

By way of the Merritt Parkway, then the George Washington bridge and New Jersey Turnpike, the Baltimore Harbor Tunnel and finally the Throughway, it took me the allotted seven hours with a comfortable hour out for lunch.

I kept a notebook in my purse for story ideas and found that, for musical themes, the back of checks torn out of my checkbook were of a convenient shape. (These, with music written on the back, sometimes turned up, confusingly, in my accountant's office.)

Once leaning over the wheel, writing notes on my miniature staff, I was surprised to see the inquiring face of a police officer at the window.

Was I all right, he wanted to know? Seeing me bent over the wheel like that—thought I had fainted.

Another time, having done several hours concentrated work in the early morning before I started out on the long drive I really gave out *en route,* too exhausted to continue driving. So I pulled up, made my coat into a bundle on the front seat beside me, doubled over, putting my head down, and tried for forty winks; only to be startled in the same way. Another policeman and another face but the same inquiry: "Are you all right?"

In mental comparisons of the various values which go into the making of a musical I had arrived at the following:

Story values: 40%

Music values: 40%

Visual effects: 20% (sets, costumes, faces, dances)

But my basic opinion was and always had been that it is music which makes or breaks a show.

I remembered days long past when I sat in a New York theatre and was charmed by *The Red Mill*.

I can still see the picturesque old Dutch windmill, its wide arms spread. Before it, dancing and clogging merrily, the girl chorus with their blond, Dutch-cut hair, their pinafores and lacy petticoats. I remember the naive Victor Herbert tunes we all liked and whistled and sang. But I don't remember the story.

The visual effects, I soliloquized, made an impact on the sense of sight, the music on the sense of sound. But the story? Not on any of the senses, but on the mind. Obviously not so deep an imprint: it faded sooner.

And yet the story is fundamental. Nothing can begin until you have it. Even in music the "program", namely the story which the music is to illustrate, is essential to many composers.

Rachmaninoff was shy about admitting that he needed a program, which was, nevertheless, the fact. He kept them to himself, as well he might, for one of them —one which gave birth to a superb composition—was the love affair of a great mountain with a little cloud which nestled on its bosom.

But to have a good story is not enough. It has to be properly constructed as anyone knows who has heard inept tale-tellers garble, confuse, belittle, or otherwise contort and spoil a good story.

Watching the New York musicals, I put my mind predominantly to this aspect: the climaxes. Spot them, time them. How long do they hold? How long is the approach to them? in other words, dramatic construction.

I carried a pencil flashlight in my purse so that I could see the faces of the watch on my wrist and of the stop watch in my hand.

I found to my surprise that often the climax came at the end of the first act. The second act was usually much shorter than the first and had little story interest. Sometimes it was just a tag with some dancing or singing or possibly a totally extraneous specialty scene, like the Uncle Tom dance in *The King and I*. And, finally, one short and usually tame scene between the two principals at the end.

In my musical the first very big scene comes at the end of the first act when the windmill goes up. There is universal jubilation because the ranch is safe from drought. Now all the gay ensemble dancing, the loud, wild chorale singing. Then the intermission. But story interest still holds because the main problem is still unsolved. What's to become of Joey? He had something else to do before he could win the Princess: kill the ogre! (Translated into the terms of this story this meant discover his parentage.)

To make sure that the suspense as to Joey's name and parentage would carry over the intermission I gave some lines to Letty's mother midway through the first act, "What if Joey does put up the windmill? It's your Poppa you have to worry about! A lost boy! With a picked-up name! And no home! And no folks! You know as well as I that your Poppa's never goin' to allow it!"

As I worked over my story, carefully timing and spacing the climaxes, I was convinced and re-convinced of its truth, its sound construction, and that it would hold interest to the end.

So much for the story.

But what about the music?

I had a friend, Adolf Koldofsky, at that time conductor of the Vancouver Symphony Orchestra, who once said something I could not forget.

"What are composers going to do!" he exclaimed. "We are about two hundred years ahead!"

"We" meant the musical intelligentsia: critics, commentators, teachers and students, conductors and publishers.

"If composers write modern music the public won't accept them. If they write traditional music the intelligentsia won't let them pass."

This was what I faced, and I knew it from the beginning. All the same I had no doubt of what I should do. I should aim my music over the heads of the musical intelligentsia at the immense, old-fashioned, melody-loving public, who would keep a show running if they liked the music; who would buy the score, set it on the piano rack at home and sing it, the whole family together.

My music was not modern music, nor did I want it to be.

So much of it lacks beauty.

This word, *beauty;* there has come to be a stigma on it.

In fact, the flight from beauty was the very core of the new movement, obviously a revolt against sweetness, tenderness, love, or any longing for them. In short, too much sentimentality. A surfeit of sweets.

Who would not agree with this? I agreed. But within reason. The new should be welcomed in—some of it, but not all; and the old thrown out—some of it, but not all. Those qualities of the old which are sound and sweet, like good bread and butter, should be kept. And kept forever.

I thought of the Common Chord.

And of that composer, the greatest of all, who said, "In it is all music."

I thought of Beethoven, ending his Ninth Symphony with twenty-six repetitions of the Common Chord.

And a small fantasy crossed my mind: if a great composer died and went to hell, and was allowed to come back to earth to hear one chord, and one only—what would it be? Surely, the Common Chord. It could be the voice of Jehovah: *I am that I am.*

But modern music makes a pretty clean sweep of all the old and accepted values. It is the same in the other arts. And in life as well.

People were to be tough and realistic. Morris Cohen wrote ". . . how will they like it when they have to do without love?"

But sex was taking the place of love. Is it an answer to his question that there are today one million people in insane asylums?

Who would have thought that it was so easy to deceive vast hordes of people? whole populations?

In music, it was Arnold Schönberg who broke the new trails.

At the first recital he gave in Germany ". . . they laughed so they went into hysterics. . . . the concert could not proceed . . . they laughed until they vomited . . . people had to be carried out."

New and different scales; tone rows; a-tonality. And all the American musical intelligentsia went along so that now, if a composer writes in the familiar diatonic scale, newspapers refer to him as dated and naive.

Reading a review in *Newsweek* the other day I came upon the words, "unashamedly nostalgic."

[50]

Shame. This is a terrific word to place beside nostalgia.

Life is full of nostalgia. You see it in the eye, hear it in the voice, notice it even in children. Since it is part of us all, it is strange to think of it as shameful and something which must be kept out of music because it is not in style.

Rimsky-Korsakov wrote, "Composers are so afraid of falling into the commonplace that they cannot be sincere."

And again, "Composers do not dare, now, to write a cantabile melody."

But these are just the musical crimes I am committing. Writing cantabile melodies, writing in the diatonic scale, writing music that is not calculated, not puzzled out to be something that has never been before, but music that is just as I feel; that is sincere; and often commonplace, often unashamedly nostalgic. And I have complete confidence that if I can only get it past critics, reviewers, columnists, musicologists to the ears of the public, they will love it, and perhaps love the show just because of it.

I find a slight encouragement in the fact that in the last decades there has been something of a reaction. People are becoming aware that something has been lost, that perhaps they threw out the baby with the bath. Psychiatrists are now declaring that there has to be love after all. Because insane people can only recover if they are loved. And children too must be loved—hugged, kissed, caressed—or else in later life something monstrous can grow out of that un-watered, un-shined-on soil.

It seems that Nature as it exists in the human heart failed to go along with the modern movement.

And if there must be love, then beauty comes again into its own. For love is that which is aroused by beauty. And when one is in love, one is enveloped in beauty. Indeed, they are the same.

Nature could have saved us from much of the upheaval. For Nature is not afraid of the commonplace or of repeating herself. She is not stingy with her delicious sweetnesses. When I return to Tyrawley in May and throw open the windows the perfume rushes in and fills the house—wistaria, lilac.

Nature is as trite and unoriginal as a pair of lovers with their classic *clichés*. It all comes around and around as regularly as the ring on the merry-go-round. And do we object? No. Unashamedly we love it. It could be music. It could be a song.

In all the critical reading I did, I looked for comments which upheld me in these rebellious opinions; and I found a considerable number.

Here was Abram Chasins, writing of the public which is "starved for melody." And an occasional drama critic putting in a plea for, just occasionally, a singable tune.

And in *Newsweek,* hard-boiled and ultra-modern as it is, the article about the night club which played nothing but very modern music from the latest Broadway shows—and was losing its clientele; then switched to the older more romantic "dated" music, and business picked up. *Newsweek* commented that the dated music would soon be used up; what would they do then, since no one was writing any more of it?

I was writing it.

I wondered why more composers were not doing the

same thing, and thought that perhaps they were. But, as Adolf Koldofsky had said, the intelligentsia would not "let it pass." Publishers would not publish it. It remained in those big boxes; and the public, which wouldn't know the difference between a diatonic scale and a tone row, would remain "starved for melody."

This is the same public that undoubtedly does know the kind of songs it likes and the tunes it can remember when it leaves the theatre, and wants to hear again—and again—and again.

It seemed a stone wall I was facing. But walls, if contemplated long enough and explored persistently, often prove to have tiny cracks in them. Into a tiny crack can sometimes be thrust a wedge—and then anything can happen.

So I don't worry about this. The music will not be modern. I hope it will be beautiful.

Seven

THE FAVORABLE REACTIONS to my story had so far been in response to my own reading or telling. Though I am no actress, as Mrs. Tuttle must have been, yet I had delivered the tale as vividly as I could. Moreover, and inevitably, I had thrown over it the glamor of my own partiality to it.

I now wanted an expert opinion of it deprived of these aids. Flat, cold, on paper. What would be the verdict?

I sent the script with a note to my friend, Luise Sillcox, Executive Secretary of the Dramatists' Guild, asking her to name a time when I could run down to New York and see her.

When I walked into her office, the script was lying on the desk before her and she immediately began pouring out information about the sort of author-producer contract the Guild was sponsoring at present. There were many practical matters to discuss.

At last I put my hand on the script and said, "What did you think of it?"

She answered briefly, "Crazy about it."

"What particularly?"

"I was carried away."

"By what?"

"Your whole approach."

"Whole approach" meant, I concluded as I drove home on the Merritt that afternoon, the mood in which I had accosted the background of my story. The American West. Those rolling plains, the highlands of this country which have been taken to the heart of the entire world as the homeland of the cowboy plus his necessary supporting cast of bandits, killers, outlaws, and gunmen.

When my eyes first beheld that world, and I quote ". . . incredible beauty . . . a clean and empty world with a slow heartbeat . . ."

The quotation is from a book of my own. I had also put the sentence in the preface of my *Catch Colt* script, just so that no one, but no one, would open those pages expecting to read of killings and gun play.

I was to find that the impact of that sentence on page four of the script was to shock every reader into attention.

Luise had probably hardly read the story or noticed where the climaxes came or failed to come; she had heard none of the music; but the dreaming quality of that "clean and empty world" word-painted on paper, had "carried her away."

How, I wondered as I turned into my driveway, can such a thing as that be caught and put on a stage?

Her last words had been, "Now we must find you the right agent."

She chose him, sent him the script and made an appointment for me to see him.

"But good heavens!" exclaimed my friend Peggy

when I told her about this (Peggy lives in New Haven and her husband is a Yale professor), "If Harold Freedman will handle your show it's as good as on Broadway. Every show he takes ends up on Broadway."

This was reassuring. An agent plays an important part in the marketing of anything, so I felt suspense as well as anticipation before the meeting.

At first glance I liked him and knew we were compatible. A quiet man, fair, of medium height, with steady thoughtful grey eyes. Personal charm, lovely manners, a cultured voice.

There was Bach on the rack of the grand piano; published plays and books on the tables. The two telephones rang constantly, interrupting us every other minute. Moreover, although he was on the eve of departure for England, he had carefully read the script and remembered everything in it.

The last part of our talk took place in a taxicab which was bearing him to another appointment and me to my club.

I have often looked back to that first visit (a good many were to follow), remembered his criticism, and realized that he has been proven right in every instance. Such understanding of dramatic values as well as of play construction is extremely rare.

I had been worried about the boy and girl love affair. Was it too sentimental? Perhaps slushy? But he disagreed. "That is one thing which has a definite value: the warmth, the feeling. . . ." and I remembered how, just occasionally on stage or screen, one becomes aware of love, real love, and the audience is spellbound! How potent a thing. I had hardly, consciously, tried for it—but there it was! He recognized it on paper.

I had been worried about the plot mechanics, the rather complicated, detective-like searching of the boy's past. "But no," said Freedman, "All that holds interest. It builds, step by step." He turned a page and frowned. "But if that old man is to be the butt of those comedians. . . ." He shook his head.

"Oh, he won't be!" I assured him. There would be a little spoofing, but in a friendly way. I registered the intention to be very careful on this point.

"You've thrown away the surprise element, I see." he looked at me with polite question. "You did that on purpose, I suppose?"

"Yes—I have no faith in really surprising an American audience. They're always ahead of you. Besides, even if you do, the scene is over so quickly. . . ."

"But then it leaves your story rather slight in the second act." he turned pages, glancing here and there.

Surprised, I disagreed, feeling that the story was solid throughout.

I was to find that when I got into making a more detailed script of the second act, almost unconsciously I made it stronger. I delved deeper into my characters, actually shifting the main issue, so gaining another dimension. The first act dealt with MOTION, culminating in the windmill. The second act dealt with E-MOTION, as Joey looked into his own heart and found that, in truth, not even he himself considered that he was a fit mate for Letty, and sang:

I'm no fitten man for you—I know it now for sure.
You and I can never be the same.
For you got a family and I got none,
No father nor mother, not even a real last name.

[57]

"The principle trouble with this play will be," said Mr. Freedman thoughtfully, "that it is Americana."

"Of course."

"And the vogue for that is past."

This surprised me. I thought Americana would always be good as a background for musicals—the real places of this country, colorful because strange and unknown to most people. I remembered *Little Old New York,* a movie. Had not that been a stage musical too? And *Louisiana Purchase?* And *Missouri?* And *Oklahoma!* breaking all records? Why should not every state of the Union have its own musical containing authentic talk and background and at least a touch of authentic history? It would remain filed away in the archives of the State Universities, ready to be brought out and revived for the edification of students and general public. Such musicals could become classics like the Gilbert and Sullivan plays.

"What about *Oklahoma!?*" I asked.

"That was popular then. It could not succeed now. Could probably not even get backing."

Another stone wall.

"But," he continued, "this sort of thing may come back, it goes in cycles. Now, here is something else you have done which makes it very difficult for me to sell this: you've done it all yourself. Story, play, lyrics, music. We sell entirely on names. The NAME of the original book— in this case there is none."

I thought of *Pygmalion* and muttered, "I see what you mean."

"And the NAME of a famous composer, like, for instance, Frederick Loew or Kurt Weil."

"Yes, I see."

And the NAME of a big Broadway writer to arrange the book, as Hammerstein arranged *Green Grow the Lilacs* and made *Oklahoma!* out of it."

"Yes. . . ."

"And the NAME of a famous lyricist for the songs. If I had four big NAMES like that, I would have something to offer a producer. That is what they buy. NAMES. . . ."

"Whereas, in this case," I summed up, "You don't even have one name that is really a Broadway name— only a literary name."

"Exactly," he agreed. "And they aren't the same at all. Broadway and books don't meet."

"What about a big name star? The lead?" I suggested.

"That's your only hope. Or it would be, if there was a big name star on Broadway today who could sing and act this part. But you have a male lead. There's no one who could do it."

I could only stand and stare at him as he delivered this final blow. He continued slowly and impassively to turn the pages of the script. He paused. "You've got one very good scene here," He allowed himself a bright look and a smile. ". . . in the second act, near the end . . ."

It was the scene of The Swedes. The Swedish lumberjacks who had been invited down from the mountains to attend the picnic. It was written now only in outline and I had let my imagination run riot: the big, bearded men riding into the scene on top of a caboose, leaping off; and the wild dance that followed during which one big fellow drags off into the woods a little dancing girl literally by the hair of her head—the humor of this would be that it would be a life-size limp doll with long blonde hair which he dragged away.

Freedman continued, "A scene worthy of the biggest Broadway choreographer." He turned away as if actually embarrassed to give praise.

"Superb," he finished in a low voice.

I cheered up. "And of course," I said, "this doesn't give any idea of the music."

His face became guarded again. He knows nothing of my music.

"And of course it's the music that makes or breaks a show," I continued.

"Not any more" he replied firmly. "It used to be, but it's not now."

I was so shocked by this that I repeated the remark and talked about it to other theatre-wise people, especially my artist friend, Aroldo du Chène, who is a conductor *manqué* if ever there was one; he knows every piece ever written and every conductor who ever waved a baton.

He shouted, "He's right! But why? Because they don't get *music* any more. Composers aren't writing it. They're just throwing together notes that add up to cacophony! Just get some singable tunes on the stage in a musical and it would put the show over fast enough!"

But when Freedman made this remark to me I stood in silence for a few minutes, thinking. Here was confirmation of what I had feared.

My music was not modern.

This probably would prove the greatest obstacle of all.

"Big names," I said finally, "I can see they would get

a show into a theatre and an audience into the seats. But, alone, they cannot provide an evening's entertainment. If not the music, what will do that?"

"The way it is mounted. Effective theatrical scenes. Dances. And the stars themselves—dramatic situations for them. And the singing climax." He flipped through the last pages of my script and looked up at me. "In the last years, always that. More and more important. *The singing climax.*"

He closed the script, and in his bright, pleasant, polite manner (which is, nevertheless, completely pessimistic) half extended it to me, half held it back, and said, "I'll talk about this with producers—if you wish."

Hesitantly I took the script. "Well. . . . if you would. . . ."

Driving home, I thought it all over.

"Talk to producers." Of course, that was the way it would be done. No producer is going to *read* a script, even if offered by Harold Freedman.

They foregathered, so Luise had told me, at a summer resort in Maine and talked over the coming theatrical season. What was offered, who would produce what. Big producers had their shows lined up for years ahead. They had their favorite stars, writers, designers, choreographers. Also "ideas" of their own or of their associates to start the whole thing off. Why should they open their arms (or stages) to a newcomer and a rank outsider? One heard that there was, quite definitely, a little *clique* of them; almost a monopoly of the Broadway stage.

Still—Freedman had said he would talk to them. I wondered how the conversation would go and presently was improvising:

[61]

Freedman:	It's laid in Wyoming . . . Americana of course . . . a ranch . . . cowboy lead.
Producer:	Who's the playwright?
Freedman:	Mary O'Hara.
Producer:	Mary O'Hara? Who's that?
Freedman:	Who wrote *My Friend Flicka.* You've read it—or your children have.
Producer:	Oh, *that* Mary O'Hara . . . well she can write books but can she write a play?
Freedman:	It's a good little story, with a real heart interest.
Producer:	Who's doing the music?
Freedman:	She's done it.
Producer:	The music too! Is it any good?
Freedman:	I don't know. I haven't heard it. But she says it is."
Producer:	What kind of music?
Freedman:	The old-fashioned kind I imagine —tunes.
Producer:	Oh, *tunes!* Tunes are all right. If they're good.

(Somebody with a bass voice begins to roar "Old Man River"—

Someone else chimes in with a Romberg tune.)

The verdict, I imagine would be, Well. . . . no. No Americana.

But on the end of my journey it was the singing climax I was thinking about. There was no singing climax in my play.

[62]

I was stimulated rather than disheartened by this. It was not like the other tabus and vetoes blocking my way. Something could be done about a singing climax. It could be written.

Already the first steps toward this were beginning in the far-down depths of me. Melodies. What themes did I already have waiting? Who would do most of the singing? So far, my old man did not sing. I had felt him too far away, too lost in his dream of hunting for the little boy, too completely detached from here and now to be fit to open his mouth and sing . . . . perhaps he would have to sing.

That night I put in a long distance call to Kent in Washington and told him all that Freedman had said about NAMES.

It happened that he was just leaving for California on Air Force business that would take about a week. He said he could take a few days' leave afterwards and see what could be done in Hollywood about finding a producer for *Oh Wyoming!*

"You have no project," he was told. "You cannot sell, because you have nothing to offer. NAMES is what producers buy. You have none. The merit of the play has nothing to do with it. Even if it is potentially a hit. Even if, provided it got on the stage, it actually would be a hit and everyone knew that, still it could not be sold. You have no project."

Merit has nothing to do with it.

So he had said. I did not believe it. Not in the long run—the long, long run. Looking way ahead, I was convinced that the thing of supreme importance was that I, as creator, should bring into being this small piece of Americana, this few dollars' worth of pleasant, lightsome entertainment. And it had to have merit. It had to be good.

I continued to write and work as if I had never heard of NAMES.

Eight

AT A PARTY a young lawyer told me that a group of men he knew wanted to finance a musical. He had heard of mine, he knew my books, why could we not all get together on this?

One does not take such remarks very seriously, especially at a party. But before the evening was over, he found me again, again brought the matter up. So I had to toss the ball back.

"What shall I tell my agent?" I asked smiling.

"Tell him you've got an angel."

"How much of an angel?"

"What would you need?"

"Oh—perhaps a quarter of a million. . . ."

"That would be a snap."

But there was a condition. I would have to produce it myself. And this, I told him, would be quite impossible.

I recounted this conversation to Luise and she said kindly, "But you don't need money—"

("Oh, no?")

"What you need is for just one big Broadway personage—just one—to get crazy about your play."

She gave it to a producer, who was a friend of hers, to read.

He brought it back to her saying, "It is fascinating reading. I knew immediately that it would never do for the stage but still, I couldn't put it down until I had read the last word."

Luise and I looked at each other, puzzled. Why wouldn't it?

"You'll get plenty of refusals," she said. "But you only need one producer. Only one to get crazy about it."

One day Luise showed me the fifteen-page contract between playwright and producer under which stage productions were now put on. It was the result of several years work by the Dramatists Guild and Harold Freedman, plus a battery of lawyers.

I took the document home with me and studied it.

What surprises! No longer could a producer override a playwright and miscast the play by putting his blond favorite of the moment into the leading role; or do what was so often done in Hollywood—dismiss the playwright then, behind his back, make such drastic changes that the whole intent and effect was altered.

I had become inured to just such abuses in Hollywood, also to the scant power and prestige accorded the author. My protection against them in this venture would be that I simply was not going to have anything to do with the production. This was practically a vow.

"But look, Luise!" I cried, "what it says here!" The contract lay on the desk between us. "That the author is bound, on request, to accompany the troupe on the road for all the tryouts, and to rewrite when necessary!"

I went on to explain, with considerable feeling, how

contrary to my intention any such collaboration was. I had, so far, never been in a stage dressing room or in the wings, or the greenroom, or up on the bridge. The personages, places, names, and ways of Broadway were unknown to me. I saw no reason why I should cross the footlights.

"As for rewriting on request, that's just what starts all the dissension."

Luise looked at me reproachfully and chided, "I can't see how an author could consider it fair just to dump the show like that, really abandon it! Authors have always complained that the producers ruined their plays. Now we have given them a contract which sees to it that they can stand by and watch over it to the end."

"Supposing there are irreconcilable differences of opinion?"

"Then someone mediates—usually Harold Freedman."

"But I never wanted to get into all those fights, to suffer the way they do."

"But won't you stand by your child? Suffer for it?"

Another producer read the play. I sent it to him. In a way, I knew him, for it was he who had said that if I would write the musical he would produce it sight unseen. This was Clinton Mack.

He came driving up the parkway from New York to see me.

"It is just the play I have been looking for. It is the play every producer is looking for. I love your people. It is Cinderella in reverse. That is, the boy is the hero instead of the girl. But the old man, Windy—he's the whole show."

This producer was an all-round genius of the stage, famous as an actor, and considered the best director in the business.

My old sheepherder, Windy, simply fascinated him. "I've heard of men going west to take up land—to seek their fortune—to find gold—but never to find a little lost boy."

He wanted to "buy" the musical and produce it, direct it, play the part of Windy himself.

This "buying" means buying a one-year option (the usual price, $5,000) after which, if he has not succeeded in raising the necessary money, the option is terminated and all rights revert to the author.

But this producer wanted no contract, no option. He wanted to begin immediately a revision of script with me. He explained that I had not made nearly enough of Windy. Windy should appear in every scene. He would predominate throughout the play.

This made me uneasy. I had decided that the story was to be primarily the romance of the young lovers with Windy providing the counter-theme or sub-plot; and at last the two plots would fuse with each other.

I did not say no right away. We had many talks and visits. We plotted and planned. He loved the music; stood behind me as I sat at the piano and plaintively howled the words. He was charming. He may have been fifty or more but he looked young, as most actors and actresses do. (How do they do it?)

Of course I talked to Mr. Freedman about it and discovered that there was a legal stumbling block. Discussions about story or script were only allowed between author and producer when they were bound by a contract, otherwise the author's title would be clouded.

Besides, I was not at all sure that Clinton Mack and I had the same concept of the play. I mentioned this doubt to him.

He met this with a quick and strong comeback "There can be only one concept: *yours*. Aren't you familiar with the Dramatists' Guild contract? No one but the author has any say about such matters."

But the issue was already closed in my mind. And vetoed. I had caught that glimpse: author seated at the typewriter, producer pacing up and down the room, author taking dictation from the producer like an amanuensis—as it was often done in Hollywood. But I had left all that behind me twenty-five years ago. It was working entirely alone in my own writing room without anyone looking over my shoulder that I had written my novels and made my name.

Mr. Mack saw my doubtfulness and did all he could to reassure me but by now I had begun to be afraid of him—even to lose sleep! Losing sleep was no part of my plan. I knew he was a man of iron determination. I think he would have got his way about everything, on the grounds, of course, of my being a newcomer to the stage.

Once again I followed my instinct to run away from trouble.

In a friendly note, reiterating my feeling that we had such different concepts of the story that collaboration would be impossible, I said good-by.

At about this time I had another nibble.

My Friend Flicka, fearfully and wonderfully serialized (not by me), was appearing on N.B.C. television.

The other television circuit, C.B.S., got in touch with me asking if I had any more *Flicka* material which was not tied up. I answered that I had not. They wrote again—any western material? I told them about *Oh! Wyoming!*.

There followed a flurry of telephone calls and letters; the script was sent them, then musical numbers. Freedman definitely pricked up his ears. Everything hung in the balance for a while.

They asked for time. Freedman is always on the alert about this. He gives them just so many days and no more. Then they wanted to send everything out to the Coast. Then they changed their minds.

I received the script back, then the music. Was it because the music was not modern? Perhaps.

Constantly probing (mentally) those walls which blocked my advance toward production, I realized that twice I had got the script into the hands of producers who had disproved my contention that producers can't read —for they had read it. These two were Jean Dalrymple and Clinton Mack.

Both of these were or had been actors. It seemed to me quite possible that actors were used to holding scripts in their hands (and did not fling them on their desks, looking at them with horror as producers did). They read them, studying the situations, trying out the lines. Actors were, quite possibly, always looking for good parts for themselves, and if they found one (as Clinton Mack had found Windy) would move heaven and earth to get the play produced. Actors might be important allies for me.

Unfortunately I knew no actors or actresses.

I wondered if Mr. Freedman had managed to get any producer actually to read the script. I thought not. I suggested a name to him: a producer who might have known of me through a mutual friend. He would try, he said; then reported that this producer begged to be excused from reading it, since he was so well supplied with plays for years to come that *Oh! Wyoming* would be no use to him even if he read and liked it.

Making an experiment on my own, I wrote a personal letter to Rodgers and Hammerstein, asking if I should submit the script. After all, I can be sure that one or more children in nearly everyone's family, has read *My Friend Flicka*—which can serve not only as an introduction but a recommendation for anything written by Mary O'Hara.

But the polite letter received in answer, begged to be excused on the same score. They had so many productions lined up ahead, it would be useless to acquire another.

No cracks in this wall.

Though I was quick to follow up any production possibilities, yet I continued to feel that the important work was to complete the play.

Kent and I discussed the accompaniment of the songs. Did it have to be orchestral? Or would piano do? Possibly two pianos?

Kent never urges me, but he was eager for a regular theatre or "pit" orchestra of twenty-two pieces.

I remembered him as a little boy, always so anxious to hear orchestras that I was hard put to find concerts for his Saturday afternoons.

I decided to make an experiment: have just one of my songs orchestrated and performed, and discover how much that added to its effectiveness. Also, discover how much it would cost.

[71]

I had no intention of investing money in the show. This was practically another vow.

Those who invest in Broadway are rich people who like to gamble and are fascinated by the stage. Win or lose, they have their fun. And I have heard that this often works out well, taxwise.

In a way, all that I own really belongs to Kent, or will some day. I inherited moderately from parents and grandparents. Twice I had lost nearly all, twice made it back. I was not going to risk it again. This orchestration would be just one experiment. Aside from buying the musical scores of *Brigadoon, South Pacific, Oklahoma,* and others, records by the dozen, there had not so far been any disbursements to speak of.

My New York music publisher put me in touch with Jack Mason, a professional orchestrator of dance band music, and a very fine one. He came to my house and we spent an afternoon in the music room with the grand piano and the song, "I Have a True Love," a haunting melody written in Bolero time. We played it, first one, then the other, discussed how it should be arranged, argued a bit. . . . shouldn't this chord be minor rather than major?

He took the music away with him and while he was making the orchestration Kent, in Washington, was arranging for a performance.

All the services, Army, Navy, and Air Force maintain full brass and string bands. They perform continually in the interest of Public Relations.

Kent asked the Colonel in charge of the Air Force band, to advise him about engaging a small professional orchestra. But the Colonel said, "Oh, let's keep it in the family."

So it was decided that a ninety piece orchestra would be used, provided they approved of the orchestration.

Counting back on the long chain of cause and effect I conclude it must have been *Flicka* that got me this great favor.

The orchestration was finished, sent to them, they approved it.

Wonderful moment when, in Washington, I heard that orchestra perform my Spanish song; when Colonel Howard, the conductor, came to my seat and said, "A good little commercial number;" and when, days later, again at home at Tyrawley, I put the record on my Hi-Fi with friends present to listen, and saw first one, then another rise from her chair, extend her arms, and float off with cries of delight.

The cost of having this one song orchestrated and the parts extracted by a professional copyist was in the neighborhood of $400. I did arithmetic to discover how much more it would have been if all those ninety musicians of the orchestra had been paid by me.

How much more, again, if all the music of my show had been orchestrated and performed.

In *South Pacific,* there were forty-nine musical numbers. In *Oklahoma,* thirty-nine. In *Brigadoon,* twenty-eight. I could see already that *Oh! Wyoming* was going to have fully as many.

I re-read passages of *Say Darling!* where the musical costs were estimated. Also in *Promenade Home.* In one book it named $13,000. In the other, $15,000.

I thought of my vow and decided that it is just tempting fate to make any vows at all.

From time to time both Luise and Freedman mentioned the possibility of getting the play produced at a university. This would provide a show case. New York managers could see it and, if they liked it, would take it to New York.

The general prejudice against producing originals, they explained, was not shared by the universities. They were supposed to lead in the dramatic field. They were really the highbrows of the stage—often subsidized by the state, supposed to keep the door open for unknown geniuses. If they produced an original and it was a success and went to Broadway, it gave them prestige. So they were on the lookout for good originals.

"What university?" I asked Luise, feeling forlorn and uprooted. Universities were all over the country whereas I was at Tyrawley, in my private ivory tower.

She named a number. Ann Arbor. Michigan State. Rochester. Indiana State.

I just couldn't take it seriously. The names faded out of my mind, whereas the singing climax, the hunting song loomed more and more important and immediate.

Luise and I lunched together, went to several musicals together. Coming out from one—definitely a piece of Americana and charming—she clutched my arm. "Was there a singing climax? I didn't notice."

I had noticed. I had been on the lookout for it. Singing climaxes were now interesting me very much.

Yes, there had been a singing climax but no wonder Luise had missed it—it was so short. A single line. It was there, and it was gone. No one could have recognized it or felt any emotional impact.

I would do better than that. It was working in me like yeast. Just where would it come? Of course, at the end when they are all locked in the grip of *yes* or *no*. Shall

Letty marry the man her parents have forbidden her? Or shall she send him away alone? Tag ends of the lyric sang through my ears: "We are made for each other. . . . I could never love another. . . . if he leaves he must take me. . . . if he goes, I cannot stay!"

Driving on the highways, I pulled up by the roadside, drew out my checkbook, and wrote lines of melody.

Nine

KENT'S NEXT ASSIGNMENT was to be in Holland.

It would be for three years. Deputy U.S. advisor to the SHAPE Air Defense Technical Center at The Hague. Following this Dutch assignment, the probabilities were he would be returned to Washington.

Looking forward to that return and dreading the arrival in this crowded city with wife and two little boys and no place to live, Kent now began to look for a house. If he bought one before he left for Holland, it could be rented until his return. The rent would pay for a houseful of furniture.

I promised that if he bought a Washington house I would do the same.

He found his house, bought it, rented it to a brother officer. A few weeks later I found a treasure of an old house in Georgetown, most tempting to one who loves to remodel. It was about to tumble down and the price, consequently, was low. It had a little white picket fence across the front and a garden on each side to separate it from its neighbors.

Having inspected this at three one afternoon, I was

the possessor of it before that day was done and was wondering what I should do about a piano.

I could hardly expect the Mason and Hamlin to accompany me via bridges, tunnels and expressways on my trips between Tyrawley and Washington. But it had spoiled me for anything but the best.

I went hunting in Washington and found an old warhorse of a Steinway concert grand, rebuilt completely as to works. Oh, those long, long bass strings! What a roar! Richer even than the Mason & Hamlin.

There remained the necessity of getting it into that upstairs front room which I had selected for my Washington studio. Because it had one wall covered with old and beautiful pine paneling; two other walls filled with tall narrow Victorian windows. And an old floor. It should be all bare. No hangings or cushions to muffle the sound. Just venetian blinds at the windows.

There was a good deal of talk at that time about President Truman's piano which had fallen through the floor at the White House. This had brought about an examination into the condition of all the wood, and the final result was the restoration, remodeling and redecoration of the entire building at a cost of about three million dollars.

My studio floor certainly looked frail. So I summoned architectural engineers. The examination and specifications which emerged decreed that first the outside north wall of the house must be removed so that a new steel beam could be inserted horizontally at floor level. What actually was at present holding that floor into the walls no one could imagine. Then there must be new joists all the way across. The kind of hard wood was specified, also that there must be no knots in it. Then new bridges for the joists. Again, no knots. Then, if I still wanted the old floor boards, a complete floor of plywood must be laid under them. Every step, every foot of wood, must be inspected by the Georgetown building inspectors.

There remained one difficulty. It was quite impossible to get that piano up the narrow staircase, nor was the roof so made that the piano could be let down to a window from above.

But I found that a tractor could hoist it from the street, deprived of its pedals and legs, of course, and thickly wrapped in quilts.

The whole street was interested when the big moving van and tractor arrived. The tractor stretched out its claw, seized the piano, and drew it out of the van.

I was watching from that front room above. Five men from the moving company had removed the sash and frame of the tall Victorian window, and stood ready, waiting to receive the piano when it should be thrust in.

They were superb physical specimens, handsome as only Negroes can be. They were dressed in spotless light gabardine uniforms and knew exactly how to place themselves, how to balance, how to brace their limbs, how to bend, slightly crouching, how to stand motionless with outstretched arms so that the immense piano, entering the window edgewise, just missing the sill, could slide comfortably to rest in their embrace, be guided, lowered to the dolly, and wheeled into place.

It was a sculptured group—heroic size. Watching, I wished that a sculptor could have been present. I thought of the Laocoön which stands in the Louvre: the mighty, bearded father, the three sons, all bound and writhing in the grasp of the boa constrictor that wraps them around.

Into my house now came old furniture, picked up here and there. And at last Hosannah Faison, glorious name, glorious large, comforting person, who sang as she worked, and always took a few flowers home with her at night.

With Hosie, there entered my house wisdom and patience; gentle, unhurried resignation; all contained in the soft, murmuring song.

Now I could begin at the piano as early in the morning as I wished. Because of the gardens on each side of the house, no one could hear. So I thought.

They heard. But they did not complain. Instead, whenever I met neighbors on the street or they dropped in to call, I heard those most reassuring words—beautiful music.

I knew it was beautiful as I wrote it. I wondered if it would help at all to breach that impenetrable wall which blocked my path with the decree, *no long melodies.*

In the spring I returned to Tyrawley and wrote the singing climax.

It took all summer. It was twenty pages of music. Joey and Letty made their plea for mercy, to be allowed to love one another. The parents refused, argued, pled, expostulated, and the whole cast, as a chorus, shouted their opinion, gibing and scoffing.

To jump ahead a few years—when the show had a week's run at the Lincoln Theatre in Cheyenne, the theatre owner said to Kent, "When I have shows running here I never stay to the end, I get home as fast as I can. But with this show, I don't leave the theatre. I wait to hear that last number once again." And at the Cheyenne newspaper office one of the editors said—and the word went around—"I think that "Catch Colt" song at the end is the finest music I've ever heard in a musical."

Ten

IF PEOPLE ARE NEWS (and newspapers say so, so it must be true) then every association of people, even two, is a story. And the story begins when you begin to look for your associate.

Could anything be more difficult? Whether you are looking for a business partner or a housekeeper or a spouse to companion you for life or a teacher before whom you must abrogate all you know and all you are.

A number of people are now going to enter this tale, to be my companions to the end. Linked to me, they create stories within the story.

Dr. Bernier, Dr. Jones, Dr. Paul, Matt, Bill, Vincent, Yohe.

Dr. Bernier was the first.

The music I had ready for the show was mostly songs and dances. I knew that there was also needed background music and interludes to cover scene changes, all of which bind the show together and make it, from start to finish, one.

I had never thought of doing this "glue" myself. I knew that there were firms of professional musicians in

New York who did this, using the thematic material given by the composer. It was immensely important work and I did not think I had the musical know-how to do it.

I was even doubtful, on many points, of accuracy and orthodoxy in the harmonizing of my melodies and felt that right now, before I got nearer the completion of my score, I ought to have a teacher to whom I could take my work for criticism and, if necessary, correction.

As a rule, beginners are over confident rather than the reverse, so it is surprising that my abilities as a composer had reached their present level without my knowing it.

It harks back to childhood.

We were, as I have said, a musical family and a large one of several generations; and as soon as a new child entered the group he or she was appraised and judged as to his musical potentiality. Did the baby's eyes roll in the direction of the piano when someone started to play? Did a look of wonder and curiosity dawn?

But because no favoritism must be shown, if he is rated high he must be held back so that the others will not be discomfitted. It is the least of the siblings who must be reinforced, encouraged, and protected. The swiftest must be hobbled. If he is an eagle, clip his wings.

In the case of Rachmaninoff, as I had learned from his biography, the musical child was treated differently.

At the age of four he was seated at the piano, playing little pieces by ear. He was then methodically taught by his governess for several years. He was then taken from his home and put in what might be called a tutoring school together with three or four other musically gifted boys. These were his companions, rivals, pace-makers. Their entire lives were oriented to music. Their host, headmaster, and drill master was a fanatical lover of and connoisseur of music, a man of importance and standing in the musical world of Moscow.

The best masters were engaged for them. They played in ensembles, went to concerts, all the musicians of Moscow visited the house, examined the boys and made prognostications as to their probable future careers. They were already recognized members of that musical world.

They were compelled to work. Rachmaninoff speaks of his incurable "laziness," no doubt that classic "wool-gathering" when he tended his sheep in those distant pastures which lay about the shores of the great reservoirs of his inspiration.

Piano practice began in the early, dark, shiveringly cold mornings—the master standing at the door dressed in his long flannel underwear, ready to crack the whip.

Trained in such a way as this, any young musician would soon know his powers, and what he was entitled to expect of himself.

In my early training the difficulty was that the things I wanted to do, simply *had* to do, were quite different from the things I was told to do.

Holding my hands just so; scales and scales and scales; struggles to read notes, learning from them disgustingly simple, childish, tinkling things;

Never a thrilling, deep bass note; or a strange, scalp-prickling chord; or, (slipping off the chair to reach with my foot) the loud pedal with all its mysterious reverberations.

It was no doubt the memory of this that caused me to put in my first published group of children's pieces the deep bass note, the strange chord. And I can still see that tiny girl's face (a second grade piano student) and the big eyes looking up at me, spellbound, as she said, "I like your pieces because they're easy but they *sound* grown up."

As well as doing what was unpleasant I was forbidden to do what was pleasant.

All that playing by ear, "stealing" everyone else's pieces, or just making things up; spending hours at the piano, making strange sounds, mostly deep bass fifths, driving everyone else crazy. . . .

Mary—fooling at the piano.

I was disapproved of by every member of the family. I suffered, but accepted the verdict. I still do. If, in a family group, I am asked to play, my hands are helpless lumps of wood.

On those rare occasions when I was spoken to as if it were true that I had musical possibilities, it was in the form of a lecture, and a heavy one. Usually the word genius would be used, but somehow made to sound more wrong than right. Other words, such as "serious responsibility" and "obligation" and "duty" would be coupled with it, the whole coming over to me as a scolding. At best, a sermon.

One never escapes the patterns of childhood.

When, in Washington, I looked for a teacher, I had the timid attitude of one who expects to be set at five-finger exercises.

I think Dr. Bernier was very much puzzled. I claimed so little he was surprised to find I had done so much. So was I.

This first, all-important association was made as follows.

Standing in church one Sunday, prayer-book in hand,

I was wondering desperately how I would find this teacher, this associate, whom I now needed. I knew almost no one in Washington. I had not a clue to guide me, not a single lead.

That was when I thought of the yellow pages of the telephone book. They say you can find anything you want in them.

Turn to the page where it says MUSIC in pretty big type, then run your finger down a little and you will find TEACHERS. Or possibly STUDIOS. And. . . .

And while I was thus diverting myself, holding my prayer-book, unconsciously I was listening to some very beautiful organ music that came from the choir loft up in the back of the large Catholic church.

Presently the train of associated ideas was complete.

Organists. Always fine musicians. They know everything about harmony. Most of them teach. My first harmony teacher, the very first to forbid me the consecutive fifths, had been the organist of my father's church.

I had been feeling that to find the proper teacher would need a real miracle or a world of luck.

Well—here they were, both miracle and luck. For I found out that the organist I was listening to was Conrad Bernier, graduate of the Paris Conservatory of Music; also teacher of fundamentals of harmony and counterpoint in the Music Department of the Catholic University of America in Washington, D.C. He had been teaching there ever since coming from Paris, twenty-five years ago.

How and why he became so interested in my play harks back to his own youth as a student in Paris. While studying Bach assiduously *en route* to becoming an organist, he was passionately interested in the theatre. This was his diversion. His friends were theatrical men. He haunted the stage, the pit.

So now he slapped his hand down upon my script with enthusiasm and exclaimed, "I am as interested in this as you are!"

I brought my work to him in the choir-rehearsal room at the Rectory of the church. Even the Rector became interested in what we were doing, would stop now and then beside our work table and ask, "How's it coming?"

One day Dr. Bernier said, "But who is going to write all the rest of the music? The interludes? Background music?" and I explained that I would get New York professionals for that.

"Why do you not do it yourself?"

"I have never thought that I could."

"You have done more difficult things." (By this time he had examined most of my compositions.)

"Have I really?"

"Much more difficult. Besides, music of a New York professional composer is not going to unite very well with *your* music. Have you thought of that?"

I had not.

"You must do it yourself. You want to continue working at music; why not this? I will help you."

Dr. Bernier was never one to do things the easy way. If there was a choice, do the difficult thing.

"Don't make things easy for your singers, make it hard. Are you worried about the high C's for the sopranos? Don't worry about that. They can all sing high C—and they love to."

I believe I have him to thank for the way my songs

soared up and up and stayed up there in the high register. It gave an exuberant and youthful effect to the whole show.

The climax of my first act was the raising of the windmill.

Now, with support like Dr. Bernier's, my confidence was rising too.

Why—after the wild song in which Joey and Letty, in a duet, sing the wind into the windmill (for at first the blades are motionless) and set it spinning—why could I not go on from there to more and more wind—and more and more clouds sweeping down, and finally the electrical storm—cracks of lightning. Everyone says you can put nearly anything on the stage.

"Certainly, the storm," said Dr. Bernier. "There are often storms on the stage. Also storms in music."

"The *Pastoral*," I said.

"Yes, and *Harald in Italy*. The huntsmen in the forests of Fontainebleau are overtaken by the storm. Berlioz."

With far more modest ideas, I suggested. "You can buy storm music. I've heard them in the movies. Many times. I'm sure they're on tape and you can buy them by the yard."

He gave me a look of pained disapproval. "But there is no reason why you should not write your own storm."

Again that strange statement: "You have done more difficult things."

This leaves me stupidly uncomprehending. I do not know what is difficult and what is not.

Certainly he did not clip my wings; he pushed and prodded me, lifted me up and pointed me on.

Of compliments he gave me plenty, suitably counteracted by a severe and frowning expression. (Naturally, a Professor would have to do that.)

"It is the great variety of your music that I like, also your long melodic line."

It dawned on me finally: he was not only teaching me in the encouraging way of all professors—*he liked my music*. And yet he was a musicologist and therefore one of the musical intelligentsia.

Could this mean that, at last, I had really found a crack in that stone wall?

Another day, frowning so heavily this time that I felt guilty before he opened his mouth, he said, "Your musical is the most important composition that has been brought to me since I came to this country."

One day I brought him a song. He cast that first lightning-quick glance over the manuscript, hurried to the piano, played it and gave a shout.

A shout from Dr. Bernier really thrilled me.

It was the song "If Only" which has since been called the outstanding song of the show. It is where Joey tries to propose to Letty and gets no farther than the words, "if only," endlessly repeated.

"Puccini!" yelled Dr. Bernier.

The melody is contained in the first three notes. These notes occurred by chance in a concert waltz I wrote fifteen years ago in Santa Barbara.

I saw that they had a certain yearning in them; it could be thematic for a love song. I wrote over them, on the page, "Theme for a Love Song."

And now, fifteen years later, I had remembered them, hunted them out, and built the song on them.

Sometimes, Dr. Bernier had one of his choir soloists try out one of my songs.

His soprano was married to a trumpet player of the navy band, a young Italian who had the name of being the finest trumpeter in the city.

She wanted to have a copy of my song to keep. He copied it for her.

Then he wanted to meet me and came to see me.

"When I wrote down those rich harmonies," he said, rolling out the word har-mo-nies as if he was smacking his lips over something good to eat, "I wanted to meet the composer." He held out his hand, smiling.

Feeling slightly dazed and almost as if I were sailing under false colors, I put my hand in his.

He continued, "I predict a great success for your show." He gave my hand a warm squeeze and added, "Your music is bold and beautiful."

I am sure I owe something of that boldness to Dr. Bernier. It is natural for me to go freely and boldly along the chosen road, but this road is now leading me into strange territory, and at every step I hesitate.

As for "beautiful"—this, the dangerous word, the forbidden thing, keeps coming to me from many sources: from performers, that is, not from musicologists. (Frank Scimonelli was a performer.)

And it reminds me of something I read about Toscanini. Expecting a visit he inquired about the man who yes, I understand that, but is he a musician?"

I took the tapes of some recordings of my songs to the Gotham Recording Studios in New York to have them put on discs, and sat in the small room watching and listening while the engineer worked with the big reels and wheels and panels of dials.

The faces of these young engineers are to such an ex-

[89]

tent poker faces, one wonders how it is possible for human beings to look so blank.

Suddenly his eyebrows shot up. His mouth opened wide, "But this is *beautiful music!*" he exclaimed.

With animation he questioned me about it. What was it going to be? How far had I got with it? He ended with the words, "We don't get this kind of music here to work with."

What startled me was the change in his manner toward me. The sudden respect, almost deference. It embarrassed me.

This work with me had its difficulties for Dr. Bernier.

The English critic, Gray, writes, "It is undoubtedly very difficult to write good light music."

If so, I thought, there is merit in doing it, and it is worthwhile.

A musical comedy is light music, so-called "popular"—a word which means not only "for the people" but also "well-loved."

It could be light in parts, classical or semi-classical in other parts.

Dr. Bernier liked my long melodies, my cantabile passages, and many of my "rich" harmonies; but he is a classicist in his tastes, his conviction, in his very soul. He left the simple, childish, and immature behind long ago. And in many places I was as immature as a hurdy-gurdy. And sometimes he could not pry me out of it.

"But why repeat and repeat and repeat this little tune? You've given it once."

"Well—because it *is* the tune," I answered stubbornly, remembering Charles Covert who said, "I admit that if there's a tune I like, I want to hear it again." And when I answered, "Of course, so do I." he went on, "and again and again and again. . . ."

And I rememberd one of the most popular tunes in *My Fair Lady*, repeated no less than eight times: "A Little Bit of Luck"

Dr. Bernier said, "No! No! Just a touch of that! Play Ravel's "La Valse!" Notice how he does it!"

"I know how he does it."

"But this is really vulgar."

At that, I gave way.

But on the use of the dominant seventh chord I could not give way. "Why don't you like it here?" I insisted.

"It is so banal," he said.

Banal.

Yes. I could see that. But this was popular music. It was quite proper for it to be banal. I would not yield.

But be reasonable now, I told myself, not too much schmaltz.

I finished the "glue." There was really nothing to that.

I wrote the storm, script and music. Then capped it with a rainbow (lovely rainbow music) then capped the first rainbow with a second; then a third. Three rainbows arching over that spinning windmill. Not a soul on the stage. This, the drama of the elements as I called it, I thought was going to be a real sensation. I had seen it often in Wyoming. I was sure it had never been seen on stage before.

The excitement of the work almost consumed me.

I wondered if even the *Pastoral* or *Harald in Italy* could have been so exciting for the composer, for in my storm, with every crash of the music I also had visual effects—lightning splitting the darkness of the stage. All this must be described in the script, carefully timed to synchronize with the music. And wind effects. And rain pouring. And with all the wild noise (when orchestrated this would be trombones and trumpets and timpani all together) there was the windmill, high in the stormy sky, spinning so fast you could not see the blades. Over all that: the slow dawning, and burning, and at last fading of the three rainbows.

In the spring Kent's orders came and he went overseas with Deirdre, Jonathan, and Richard.

I returned to Tyrawley and made my old man open his mouth and sing.

> Just about so high, I think he'd be
> A tow-headed boy, like Joseph, like me.
> Eyes very trusting, that innocent blue,
> When he looks up, they smile at you.

And then the chorus, in which the two other sheepherders join.

> I'm (he's) hunting a little boy!
> Has anyone seen my (his) little boy?

I found the themes for it in a theme book twenty years old. New music grew out of that—all I needed and more. At the piano I had the script on the rack beside the manuscript. The words made themselves as I went along.

[92]

Sometimes, with amusement, I remembered, as I wrote, the day when I stood in church and thought that perhaps I might find a good teacher in the yellow pages of the telephone directory. Well, I had not only found one, I had found that the forbidding stone wall did have a crack in it.

So—get a wedge into that crack—and anything could happen.

Eleven

IN ONE OF MY taxicab conferences with Harold Freedman, he said, "It would be a help if you had the music recorded."

The cab stopped and he opened the door.

"Do you mean *all* the musical numbers?" I asked as he stepped out. "There are forty-five."

He lifted his hat and said brightly, "Some do."

I had stopped over in New York on my way from Tyrawley to Washington in the fall of the year.

Continuing down the New Jersey Turnpike the wheels under me argued the question of the recordings. First every musical number would have to be orchestrated.

The books said the cost would be from twelve to fifteen thousand dollars.

To undertake such an expense now, when production was uncertain, would be ridiculous. I had been wondering for some time if it would be too difficult for me to do them myself. All university students who major in music are obliged to take orchestration along with theory and harmony.

There was the question of time. It would no doubt

take me a year, perhaps two. But what difference? There were no serious offers of a production as yet (though one might come at any time). Meanwhile I could be doing this fascinating work. I was sure it would be fascinating.

Dr. Bernier took me to the Catholic University and introduced me to Dr. Paul, head of the Music Department, teacher of piano, musical director and conductor of the university orchestra; and virtuoso in the great art of managing everybody and everything.

Dr. Paul introduced me to Dr. Jones who taught orchestration.

It was generally agreed that Dr. Jones knew more about orchestration than anyone else. He was one of those geniuses who could take any instrument (or any gun) apart and put it together again.

A very quiet, slow-speaking, mild-mannered man with a slight stammer; never upset, never hurried, *never wrong*.

I wondered whether Dr. Bernier's open-mindedness about traditional music as against modern music was a policy of the University or personal to himself. I could not find out from anything Dr. Paul or Dr. Jones said. But all the teaching used the classics as examples: Mozart. Haydn. Beethoven.

Dr. Jones advised against my going into the classes —he thought it would be very slow for me. Better to take private lessons from him in his office there at the University.

A lesson of one hour. One can't get much in that, so I took two-hour lessons once or twice a week, and at home I worked all the time.

In addition to the hours with Dr. Jones, there were hours spent in the instrument clinic, the large rehearsal hall full of instruments: strings, wind, brass, two grand pianos, harp, timpani, etc. Here, instruction was given twice a week and a little orchestra was formed in which I played first violin.

I took to orchestration like a duck to water. It seemed to me, in a way, easier than the piano, for instead of having only ten fingers to get your effects with you have dozens of instruments.

The memorizing of ranges, of timbres, of transpositions, of new and different clefs, was arduous and toilsome, but the thrill of having always an instrument at hand to make the exact sound you want made up for everything.

Dr. Jones said, "You are doing well . . . you are doing *awfully* well . . . you grasp it with understanding. . . ."

"If I were in the class, what mark would I get?" I asked hopefully.

Dr. Jones, who never spoke a light or careless word in his life, placed one hand over his eyes for a few moments.

I expected him to say A, in spite of occasional carelessness, the forgetting of accidentals or clefs or running out of range or trouble with the transposing instruments, but when he removed his hand he said B.

He will not overlook one single error.

I continued seeing Dr. Bernier whenever I felt I needed to talk something over with him and often a casual word or two from him opened up a whole new vista to me and, possibly, set me off on a new marathon of work.

"Don't you like this part, Dr. Bernier?"

"Yes, I do. So much so that it seems a pity that it is so short. The listener could stand much more of that theme —not exact repetitions, of course, but in development."

It was not like a professional directive, it was just a smiling friendly casual remark, and instantly I was aware that through my dread of criticism on the score of being too sentimental I had thrown away a potentially popular theme.

This theme was the melody to which I have now given the separate title of "Lonely Plains" (it is definitely nostalgic). I made it a song for Letty to sing in her all-important waltz song; also part of the waltz while she dances; also the entire final number of the show, the Exit music.

Gradually, different parts of the operetta find their place and are graded in importance as it were by their own weight.

One day I asked Dr. Bernier, "Why have you never corrected my harmony?"

"There is nothing to correct."

"But I really don't know the rules the way other composers know them."

"You compose by instinct."

(I thought to myself—evidently not as engineers built the George Washington bridge, knowing what they were doing, but as a beaver builds his dam, not knowing.)

Dr. Bernier continued, "Or perhaps you have a system of your own. There has to be a system but it does not have to be the one taught in the textbooks. Read the autobiography of Milhaud, the French composer, a talented and active composer almost from birth. He was constantly urged to study, to go to a Conservatory. At last, when he was eighteen, he did; but had to give it up. They could not teach him, he could not learn. Besides—it made him ill."

It made me ill too.

I tried it.

Dr. Bernier had continued, "If you are interested in systems of harmony, come to my class in fundamentals at the university." His face lit up. Bach and fundamentals, these were his very life.

He made a little bow. "As my guest."

I was already going to the university several times a week; I could drop in at this class without losing much time.

I began with enthusiasm.

That textbook! It had four hundred and thirty-nine pages. Masses of symbols to memorize—a veritable shorthand. There were dozens of examples of Bach: short chorales, fragments, preludes, all with the shorthand symbols underneath. We analyzed these examples, beginning at the end where the cadence was or would have been had there been one, and working back toward the beginning.

(Does one compose backward? Stravinsky, I have been told, begins in the middle and works both ways. In the writing of a story sometimes one begins at the end and works forwards. But, of course, all analysis is the reversal of creation.)

This analysis of Bach was done with the mind only, ear did not enter into it. The river of sound, of music, in my mind interfered with the work, as if the two streams, one running backwards, one forward, collided head on.

One stream had to be quenched. It was mine that was quenched. There had to be an absolutely clean slate for Bach.

With my own music killed I felt very strange. A world without music!

Then the symptoms became physical. Diminished energy and vitality; slightly squeamish; my eyesight worsened. I wondered if there was something the matter with me.

Dr. Bernier was as baffled as I. Once he asked me to go to the piano and play a simple cadence which he specified, and stood a little way off, turned to listen, while I sat there, laboriously trying to remember the exact directions on just a certain page of the textbook which should now govern the movements of each of the four fingers I was to use.

Only four! Very hard on me who always used ten and needed ten more!

He suddenly exclaimed, "It is really extraordinary how badly you do that!"

He walked agitatedly up and down the floor, and then lit on a solution. "Don't try so hard! Let it come to you!"

And I suppose that was really what for me was needed (the beaver—not the engineer). Just "letting it come to me" had given me the musical.

But I kept on with the "fundamentals" for many months. When my "trying too hard" began to give me near blackouts as I sat at the piano, I gave it up. It immediately slid out of my mind. My own music moved back into my consciousness and I regained good spirits and energy.

That was only a few years ago and I have an excellent memory, but not a trace of that theory remains in my mind.

For me, it was too late to learn.

For Milhaud, it was too late when he was eighteen.

An intimate friend of George Gershwin told me that, in his twenties, Gershwin tried to master the system he had neglected when he was younger but his piano playing suffered—he could not play. It was too late.

It should be taught very early. But not, I think, as an intellectual system to be mastered from books and exercises done at a desk. Let sound always be the guide.

In my work with Dr. Jones it was not long before we came up against my individual "system" of harmony. I had been anticipating this with some uneasiness.

Having asked me several questions which I was unable to answer, he said, "But then—if you don't know the chords, how can you write music?" He pointed to the score on the piano rack. "What chord are you going to put here?"

If it had a name, I didn't know it. I knew that several different combinations of notes would do.

Dr. Jones was waiting for an answer. Finally I said, falling back on a literary description of the sound I wanted, "Well, an active chord, a chord of great urgency."

Dr. Jones was puzzled and I was embarrassed.

"Do you know what notes will be in it?"

"I think it will be F natural, B natural, E flat, and A flat."

"How do you know that?"

"By the sound."

He seemed to have some long thoughts about this, then said kindly, "Well—that's all right too."

I drove home from my lesson asking myself, "But isn't the *sound* the whole point? Don't the textbooks emerge from the sound rather than the sound from the textbooks?"

After a few months, Dr. Jones gave me the five-voiced fugue in C sharp minor from Bach's *Well-Tempered Clavichord* to orchestrate for an orchestra of ninety pieces.

This was a big experience in my life, so exciting (as if I had the big orchestra inside me) that I walked the floor and wrung my hands. I found that I had to do it at a sitting no matter how long that sitting lasted. Over and over again I tried it, got part way, perhaps to the middle, then in exhaustion had to stop; and found that next day I didn't know where I was and had to start over. After a week of these abortive efforts, I finally did it in one day, proofread it the next day, and put it in my brief case.

Dr. Jones tilted his head, gave me that kind and quiet look, and said, "This is a good orchestration."

Dr. Jones thought that now I could begin work on my own music. I would no longer score for a symphony orchestra of ninety pieces but a "pit" orchestra of twenty-two pieces.

He listed them. Besides piano, percussion, wind and strings, there were two trombones, one tuba, and three trumpets. No horns.

I now had a piece of desperately hard luck.

It was not the right orchestra for me, or for my music.

This dawned on Dr. Jones gradually as, song by

song, piece by piece, he came to know my music. It was a year before he told me.

Fortunately, at this time I had no inkling of what was to come. I began with confidence and optimism, choosing as my first effort the Prelude which was to open the second act: a piece all color and mood, called "Midsummer Hums in the Meadows." There was a bird in it which, at intervals, gave a cry (I thought of the flute). There were bees humming, and I thought of the violins (Schubert's "L'Abeille"). And I thought of Pan with his pipes—the clarinet. I couldn't wait to begin.

Twelve

PROCEEDING IN MY WORK with Dr. Jones I saw (with relief and self-congratulation) that there was no prejudice in his musical thinking against my kind of music. Nor in the textbook he directed me to buy. Kennan's *Orchestration*. The work was all done with classical examples.

I bought one or two other books as well.

Then Dr. Bernier brought me, with a beaming smile and charming little bow, his own copy of *Principles of Orchestration* by Rimsky-Korsakov.

By common consent, Rimsky-Korsakov was the highest authority. His orchestrations (Rachmaninoff said) were "shot through with irridescent color." It is easy to see how he came by his amazing virtuosity, for not only did he have his great inborn talent but he had the job, in Russia, of supervising and bringing up to date all the naval bands. What a fund of invaluable experience!

One after the other they were brought under his command; enlarged or cut down; new instruments purchased; or *new instruments created;* hours of rehearsal to improve the individual players or alter their methods.

This went on for years until these bands became performing virtuosos, causing everyone to marvel.

This information I got out of Rimsky-Korsakov's own autobiography, *My Musical Life,* which I found in a second-hand book shop.

With all his genius and his immense creativeness, he was as humble as a child, a personality of the greatest charm.

Now that I was going to do orchestrations I felt that I was entering an assemblage of musical giants.

Since it is said that a symphony is the highest expression of the spirit of man I chose four great symphonic composers to study—particularly as to their methods of orchestrating. Rimsky-Korsakov, Beethoven, Rachmaninoff, Sibelius. I might say I devoured them, and all four at once. I read their lives, their letters, bought their pictures, had them enlarged and pinned around my music room, played their music on my Hi-Fi, bought and studied the scores of what I was listening to; and felt at last that I knew them pretty well.

Each of them, except Beethoven, admitted to having had great difficulties with orchestration; and, as to Beethoven, Rimsky-Korsakov admitted it for him, saying that many of Beethoven's orchestrations were "clumsy." And yet it is said that Beethoven worked and reworked his material endlessly—trying it this way, then that, over and over, waiting and testing, doubting and weighing.

Rachmaninoff wrote that orchestration was difficult for him and caused him much study and rewriting. He sent one of his symphonies to Respighi to be orchestrated. Respighi had learned orchestration from Rimsky-Korsakov and now, himself, was the maestro in his native Italy.

If we could see ahead of ourselves on the path of life, what trails we are going to cross, how thrilling it would be. I was now embarking on a project which, in not too many months, would cause me to cross the path—at two removes—of the great master himself, Rimsky-Korsakov. For he taught Respighi; and Respighi taught a young Italian named Marco Frascati who was now in New York; and from M. Frascati I myself was soon going to be taking lessons.

Sibelius, so said his critic and biographer (Harold Johnson), was deficient in skill in orchestrating: his work, ". . . replete with passages so clumsily scored that each instrument succeeds in canceling out another . . ." ". . . this orchestral color, a dirty brown . . ."

At such bad notices Sibelius would always withdraw the work and put it away for further revision—which sometimes took nine years!

But then the later notices came: ". . . better orchestrations . . . more long pedals and notes *sostenuto* . . . a thrilling and brilliantly conceived musical narrative . . ."

I made a mental note to remember that. But nine years!

For all of them it was necessary, in fact urgent, to have orchestras for try-outs for their orchestrations. In spite of Sibelius' failures he did have such an orchestra. It belonged to a friend of his and was at his service at any time for experimentation or practice.

Tchaikovsky wrote to the Moscow Conservatory saying that he had composed a new symphony and would like a try-out. So, please, assemble the student orchestra and get it ready for him.

All my four great composers, I learned, borrowed,

[105]

stole, took, or in one way or the other helped themselves to themes not their own.

Rachmaninoff reproached his friends that they allowed him, unbeknownst to himself, to use a theme for one of his symphonies which came straight out of Schumann.

Finlandia, that famous song-hymn, is by Sibelius in that he used it and made it famous. But the same hymn, note for note, was used and published before Sibelius by another Finnish composer, Genotz. And what old song did *he* get it from?

The five great Russian composers who were called The Five were the worst. They met in the evenings to play their work to each other, alternating at the piano or playing four or eight hands at two pianos. They bandied their themes back and forth, played snatches of "something they had heard somewhere" and used that around which to create an opera. Or one gave a theme to another, saying that he, in turn, had it from a friend who had got it from a book of Arab songs. The folk tunes of every country were, of course, anyone's to use.

Rimsky-Korsakov and The Five scorned education for musicians.

"We know what we know, by ear," he said. "All that we did was by ear."

He explained, further, that if anyone wanted to learn the textbook vocabulary, the "shorthand" symbols, musical syntax, it could all be learned in one afternoon.

He described how he would entertain his friends at the piano by playing for them, for as long as they wanted to listen to whatever came.

So no one need be ashamed of this sort of "fooling".

When I was at school the girls would get me to play on a Sunday afternoon and would lie on cushions on the floor of the big room with their arms twined around each other listening for several hours to "whatever came"—bits of opera, current songs, old ballads, improvisations. An orgy of schmaltz often accompanied by delicious weeping. Occasionally there would be a concert piece, memorized from the notes and practiced till I could play it perfectly.

All that one reads about Beethoven overwhelms one.

"The well known pictures of him," so says Grove's Dictionary of Music, "dreamy, soulful, gentle, remote, have been so idealized that they convey nothing of his true appearance."

I suppose one can trust this dictionary but it is painful to do so. Grove continues, "A short, squat man of tremendous strength, built like a bear, a wild mop of thick black hair, features that would suit a prize-fighter, rude and brutal manners, and clownishness—a man always tilted at an angle to play the fool."

What had always astounded me in Beethoven's music was the fury.

The Appasionata.

When I first heard it I said, But why is he in such a rage?

It's all there in his music: rage, and horseplay, blows and insults.

Also religion. In his writing, that pitiful prayer— Oh God! Let me soon find her who is destined to be mine, who will strengthen me in virtue.

He was not virtuous. He wanted to be; he had not the strength. Was this his inner conflict? Was this why he raged all the time?

It was also, I think, because he refused suffering. Suffering can be a door. If you go through you can gain marvels.

But Beethoven, outraged, exclaimed, "Why that might even make me unhappy! *That* I would never endure!" and lived up to it, shouting and cursing.

It is said, also, that he had charm. Women, ladies of the aristocracy, of breeding, championed and protected him. He must have had a smile. There must have been deep and glowing fires in his eyes.

Then there is that incalculable fascination of genius. Many people have traces of it. Even a little marks a man and makes it worthwhile to be near him. I have always gravitated toward genius.

It was said that when Beethoven played extemporaneously (and this was his greatest skill) he was in transport, and his face sublime.

Here and there in his music is simple sweetness, as in nature: the fresh pink, the rose, the garden; and who, walking there, will not bend and sniff? Even Beethoven. Even he might have been tender had he found her who was to have been his own, who would have strengthened him in virtue.

Frustrated in that hope, frustrated by ill health, frustrated by his dreadful deafness, and *refusing to be unhappy,* he lived in a rage, pressurized beyond bearing from within by the impossible wealth of his musical ideas, equipped with the skill of a god in assembling and shaping them, and the fury of a maniac to drive the work to completion.

Biblically, anger is equated with spirit. Who would not want to have spirit? I have seen my small grandson, Jonathan, aged four, explode like a rocket when provoked by injustice; shrieks which continued for ten minutes accompanied with great bounds into the air. Sitting on the garden bench with workbasket and sewing, I watched these fireworks without speaking. Spirit! Spirit can make one leap like that, shreik like that, blaze like that! I thought of my young stallion at the ranch, Reingold. I had seen him once in the corral putting on just such a show of spirit—what neighs and screams! His body arched and stiffened. He placed all four feet together and bounced. He lashed with wicked heels higher than his head, ears flattened, nostrils flaring, eyes fearfully rolling; a terrifying but glorious sight.

Again, it was injustice which caused this. His favorite young wife had been taken from him and corralled elsewhere.

In Jonathan's performance there seemed from moment to moment no diminution of violence. Streams of fluid poured from his eyes, his nose, his mouth.

Feeling sympathetic—all that mess on his face and he a fastidious child—I silently held out toward him a handful of tissues which I took from my workbasket. On one of his furious wheelings he caught sight of it. Not immediately, but quite soon, he shot toward me, for the moment ceased his shrieks, and pushed his face out to me. He held still while I thoroughly mopped and dried, then rushed back to that spot on the lawn for unfinished business. He was not through with the show yet—not nearly. Again he bounded, shrieked, wheeled, and wept, but the leaps were not quite so high. In a moment, I held out more tissues and again he came and was mopped. Before

[109]

he could resume, I upset my workbasket, and without a sound he began to pick up the items, one by one. When he had restored all he continued to stand there at my knee, playing with the spools. I continued to dry his face every few moments until the rivers ceased to flow. When I heard that long shuddering sigh I lifted him to my knee and he laid his head on my breast.

Beethoven remained an angry man to the last and died at fifty-six, after a horrible illness of several months during which his body swelled with water which, by tapping, was drawn off from time to time in enormous quantities.

The noisy and violent death struggle lasted two days and two nights. During this he was unconscious. Near the end, an electrical storm gathered over the city, and an awful crack of thunder ripped him, as it were, from the edge of the grave. He started up from his pillows, flung back his head and raised his clenched fist, shaking it in a final fury of defiance.

Now, having written this dreadful scene, which haunts me, I must go to the piano and play over and over again that beautiful melody in *Coriolanus* which emanated from this tormented genius.

It is the death of the king; and, yes, there is death in the music. It can be recognized—the finishment.

I have always believed music to be an exact language of the emotions. In all operatic composing, such as I am doing, this must be the first consideration: does this music, this theme, exactly express the mood or emotion of the scene or program or lyric?

One can recognize the exact emotion; each is different from every other. Despair different from grief, grief different from longing.

In all Beethoven's work there is no despair. How should there be in a man who rejected suffering?

But there is deep grief; there is sadness.

And in *Coriolanus* there is something so subtly sweet, so gentle, so humble, so wistful along with the grief that it makes the heart ache. Oh, Beethoven! After the last note, the meaning flowers out. Peace. . . .

He wrote it—so he knew it.

Thirteen

IT HAD BEEN VERY SLOW, my growth in confidence.

It was principally Dr. Bernier who gave it to me, but there were others too.

Washington is a city of music. Nearly all the Broadway musicals have their first try-outs there.

It has schools of music, universities with music departments, and consequently, professors, musicologists, doctors of music. It has a big symphony orchestra. It has the service bands.

Besides this top layer it is crammed with other musicians: children playing in school bands; boys standing behind counters in music stores and selling instruments (and playing them); boys copying for composers, or brought together to play in the orchestras of musical shows having try-outs.

They all know each other and communicate. Whenever there is a new composer he is talked over, appraised, and judged.

Talk about my show was going the rounds and I could see that it was favorable. There was respect in their manner towards me. Young students consulted with me.

The musical director of a school, asked how I found my melodies.

The answer was not easy; I was hesitant and careful. "Well, it is a search for beauty in the field of music. . . ."

"Will you please put that in plain English?"

"Well, it is an innate sense. . . ."

He interrupted. "Now you've said it. Innate. It's born in you. I always thought so."

That winter five musicals closed down on Broadway, all within a week of opening. These were all true "projects", with NAMES: stars, song-writers, authors; but the public didn't want them.

Broadway enforced its terrible terms. HIT—or out you go.

Meanwhile my musical was slowly getting into shape with no setbacks whatever. It now had roots, trunk, branches, and a small army of well-wishers helping it along.

True it had no NAMES; but perhaps by the time it was ready, there would be some handsome baritone with a NAME on Broadway who could sing the part.

And of course it was Americana. . . . but perhaps by that time Americana would be in style again.

Nor had any single important Broadway personage fallen in love with it; but that was really fortunate, since it was not ready yet.

Luise wrote me about a different way of getting a show into New York: by the back door, as it were; starting it in the west, coming across country.

If it was good and got good notices, New York producers might want it.

Actually, the idea of a western opening had been

nudging me for some time, specifically a Cheyenne, Wyoming opening. For the ranch where I had written *My Friend Flicka* was near Cheyenne, and Cheyenne claimed me as a resident.

That famous festival which Cheyenne holds every summer, "Frontier Days," crowded the town with visitors from every state in the Union, also from England and the Continent. Why not have *Oh! Wyoming!* running too for that week? Why not have the two shows somehow linked? They would not compete since the Rodeo was a daytime show and the musical an evening.

Correspondence along these lines began between me and Charlie Carey, the chairman of the "Frontier Days" committee, and he was enthusiastic. I sent him the script. He read it and liked it. The whole plan appealed to him; it was a "natural" he said. "Mary O'Hara's first musical."

I discussed all these things with Kent. The Atlantic ocean had not interrupted our communication. There were letters of course; there was also the transoceanic telephone, our talk sounding clear and close as the calls between Tyrawley and Washington.

On a visit to New York I saw Mr. Freedman who said, "Well, now you are at the Catholic University. They have a very fine drama department. Father Hartke, who has charge of it, is as good a producer as any in New York. See if they will not put on your show there. A few years ago they put on an original. A New York producer saw it, liked it, and bought it. It was a hit on Broadway."

So when I returned to Washington I went to see Father Hartke, chatted with him about it, and left him a script.

In due time I went to see him again and received the

[114]

script back from his hands. His refusal was on the score that his work there at the university had to be with the students who came there to learn drama. It would hardly be fair to them to produce a play, an original, by an outsider.

What a piece of good luck it would have been for me if, right here, where there was no prejudice against traditional music, I might also have found a producer. Too good to be true. . . .

But the reason he gave did not seem very convincing. I had begun to hear talk of rivalry and even enmity between the drama department and the music department. This rather dismayed me. If politics also was going to enter into the fate of my play!

Later, when I was again in Connecticut and had a chance to talk to my friend Peggy, I told her about this and she said immediately, "Oh yes! Didn't you know that? Why, it's that way in all universities. Here at Yale, when they had just put in the music department and we celebrated by having Drama and Music together put on a musical, they fought so we've never tried it again!"

Father Hartke was a very striking man. The kind of man, I thought, who might be a real genius. A great deal of power. And charm, too, whenever he wanted to use it.

I seem to be using the word genius quite often. If I have neglected to use it of Dr. Bernier, I here and now correct that omission.

I once said to Dr. Paul, "Don't you think he's extraordinary?" And with his usual impassive expression he answered, "He's forgotten more music than the rest of us know all put together."

And this is the one whom I demeaned, persuading

him into vulgarities, insisting on a tremolo (just like the old, trite Indian love calls) as an accompaniment to my rainbow music. And teased into writing the awkward thing for me, so that at last he grumbled, "It is not enough that I have to consent to this, I even have to write it for you."

At Christmas (this was Kent's second Christmas in Holland) I went overseas to be with them for the holidays.

This meant dinner in New York the night I left. Kay and Charles drove down from Southport to meet me at Idlewild. We dined in the airport restaurant. They put me on the plane. I had a comfortable night's sleep in a real berth and breakfast in Amsterdam with Kent.

His greatest interest was in the orchestrations. How did I really feel it was going? How many had I done? How long was it going to take to do them all? Was I satisfied?

I was very far from satisfied.

In fact, of all the work on my project, it was in the department of orchestration more than in any other that I had experienced real suffering. For I had discovered that I would never be able really to excel.

At first, when Dr. Jones said that my orchestrations were "good," "awfully good" and Dr. Bernier used such words as "fantastic" and "unbelievable," I thought these words referred to the quality of my orchestrations.

But the longer I worked, the more disturbed I got. I knew there was something wrong, a great deal wrong, practically everything wrong.

I looked at the pages of my scores, so neatly and

even gracefully written, and fell into confusion at the sight of them; they transferred to me a sickening feeling of chaos.

I worked harder. I practically knocked myself out so that I would fall on the bed and lie prone for an hour. The trouble was, I didn't know what was wrong, consequently didn't know where to apply my efforts. Questions to Dr. Jones did not help, he merely said in surprise that the orchestrations were "all right;" and always referred to the piano score from which the orchestrations were made. If that was "what you want" then the orchestrations were correct.

Those words "what you want" evaded the whole department of taste.

I feel that a student's taste must be trained. I have often had doubts about my own. And when I practically forced Dr. Bernier to say "vulgar" and "banal" it was because I had suspected it and wanted confirmation.

I suggested to Dr. Jones that since I didn't like the way the orchestration had worked out, I should change the piano score. He demurred. One must always follow the piano score.

"But since I wrote it?"

He yielded the point and thereafter I frequently changed the piano, but it always went against the grain with him.

I came to believe finally that the encouraging words from both Dr. Jones and Dr. Bernier referred to the speed with which I had grasped orchestration, not to the quality of my scores. And if I had been quicker than most beginners, it was probably because of the peculiar way in which I play the piano, making things sound more like an orchestra than a well arranged piano piece. In fact, Dr. Bernier had disconcerted me more than once by saying, when I showed him the manuscript of a piece arranged for the piano (by which I meant notated exactly as I played it), ". . . but it is not what you would call a piano arrangement."

I challenged this; he insisted. "Believe me, this is not a piano arrangement."

He was always polite but I perceived that my piano amused him. He was also a little curious—it intrigued him. Once, he took a quick step to the piano as I was playing: "What is that you did there? Oh, yes, I see."

As I proceeded with orchestration I began to understand that just what hindered with the piano arrangements, helped with the orchestral. And this is why I was able to grasp orchestration quickly.

Undoubtedly, those students who do not have this familiarity and facility with the piano keyboard, but who begin with a wind or brass instrument (and most of them do), would take far longer to grasp orchestration.

Besides, the standard expected of students was not too high. Perhaps to get a student to the point where he was not making mistakes, to where his orchestrations were "all right," put him on a certain level, abreast of a dozen or so others, and these were the successful orchestrators of Washington. I had not yet reached that level because I still had to be guided by Dr. Jones. Anyone rising above that level, I thought, must surely begin to acquire a Name. I had heard of only one: Charley Cliff.

Besides, those with whom I was comparing my scores were Rimsky-Korsakov and Beethoven.

I know when I am being silly; and I have no intention of wasting myself by attempting the impossible; so I made a mental compromise. If ever the show got moving toward Broadway, the orchestrations could be done over by some expert, perhaps Robert Russell Bennett (universally conceded to be the best). Meanwhile if my orchestrations—with or without the help of Dr. Jones or someone else—could only arrive at being "all right" they would do temporarily for whatever might come up in the way of a school or university production.

To sum it all up, Kent said: "Well then, you're not satisfied but you do think they are all right?"

This I most certainly did, because of Dr. Jones. I was sure he would let nothing pass that contained mistakes.

"Then why not have them performed and recorded here in Holland? All the prices are about a fourth of what they are in the United States."

There were good musicians in Holland. And he was there to see to it.

We did not either of us think it would be necessary to record all the music. When I got home I could select five or six numbers that I thought the best and send them to him. He would do the rest. So it was decided.

We also had much to discuss about a Cheyenne run. I had the file of my correspondence with Charlie Carey to show him. Charlie was, at this point, thinking that the production could be put on out there—amateur groups, and so on. I doubted this.

"Well, what else?" Kent asked.

"Have it made in Washington by a university," I said.

"But Father Hartke has turned it down."

"There are other universities."

"And then take the whole troupe out there?"

I nodded.

"Cost a fortune."

I explained that we might just break even; for Carey had written saying that we could count on a sold-out house for the week's performances and this would bring in about thirty thousand dollars.

It would be a gamble, of course, since we'd have to spend the thirty thousand before we made it, but Kent was all for it.

And I had the new script to show him; the music to play for him; the new scenes of the storm, the rain, and then the rainbows.

I knew perfectly well that I had put some outrageous things in the script and that there was little chance of their being in the final production, but how could I be sure? Any tendency to be cautious about such things had been taken out of me by my moving picture work.

On one occasion Rex Ingram, and I were chatting about a picture he had just finished. I had written the script for him and I happened to mention an idea I had had—a scenic effect, which I had thought of for the picture.

"But you did not put that in the script?" he said, and I saw that he looked angry. "Why didn't you?"

"I thought it would be quite impossible for you to do."

He flew into a rage and scolded me, making the point that it was not for me to judge in advance of what he could or could not do; I was there to supply effective ideas whenever I had them to give. Leave it to him to decide what he could use and what not. He then explained how he could easily have achieved this particular effect with miniatures.

He liked such things.

I had put in another scene, a "specialty," in case we ran short. It would fit in anywhere. It was a black-and-white dance, very stunning, dancers all in black leotards, bare black branches of leafless trees with black owls sitting on them; one huge, blazing white moon.

I did not forget that the script was already overwritten. It still seemed best to me to let it grow as it willed and allow the final shaping and cutting to wait until production.

When I returned to Washington I examined my finished scores. There were twenty. I selected six of the best, packaged them, and sent them to Holland.

Fourteen

CHARLIE CAREY WROTE ME from Cheyenne. "Have you records of the music? There's a great deal of interest out here. We'd like to hear it."

I answered him, Not yet but soon. For Kent was reporting that parts were being extracted and he had engaged a band leader, Dolf van der Linden, who would get the singers, the best in all of Holland.

I had sent him "Green Grass of Wyoming" already published by Sam Fox Publishing Company; "If Only," the duet between Joey and Letty; "Love at First Sight," the duet between Letty and her mother; Letty's waltz song, "Early Morning"; my favorite, "Midsummer Hums in the Meadow," the prelude which opened the second act; and the march, "The Big Hill."

That march had quite a history.

Years ago, at the ranch, there was a week when I composed three songs, determined to be very down to earth and simple and, if possible, publishable.

One was later published by Fox Publishing Company under the title of "Esperan"; it's now "I Have a True Love."

The second, with considerable revision, has become one of Letty's songs with the title, "Everything's So Different."

And the third, in two-four time, was a very simple little folk song type of thing with several verses to be sung and a quite good refrain.

In New York I took it to a publisher, Abe Richter, a tall, handsome and very well-dressed Jew who asked me to sit down opposite his desk and took the manuscript in his hands and began to read and whistle it very softly.

Presently his expression changed, he began to nod his head gently, his eyebrows went up.

His whistling was excellent. Very artistic and right on pitch.

He finished the song and put it down.

"Concert stuff, Miss O'Hara," he said. "You've brought it to the wrong place. This is Tin Pan Alley."

As I walked away I wondered why it was concert stuff. Just a little folk song thing in march time, *extremely* simple.

I offered it here and there without success. It changed its name. Several times I wrote new verses for it on different themes; at last dropped out the words entirely. It became the "Old Timers" march. Then, suddenly, "The Big Hill." In western language this means the Rocky Mountain Divide. It had always amused me, typical American humor. This eight-thousand-foot mountain range just, to the transcontinental train crews, a big hill.

Every time I heard the piece or thought of it my opinion of its merit strengthened. Someday it might be a hit and if all else failed this might go on and compensate, even, possibly, the expenditures.

I made it the entr'acte.

It was a quiet moment in Dr. Jones' small office, late afternoon; the occasion: I was just going to start a new orchestration; when gently, and with that small stammer which was just an instant's hesitation before speaking, he suggested that we shift to a different group of instruments.

He cannot have had the slightest awareness of the shattering blow he was dealing me. I was silent, my blood racing, all my pulses pounding.

He explained, "What I have given you is really a jazz band. The three trumpets and three trombones. When you first came to me I knew it was for a musical show and I took it for granted it would be the usual jazz. I am sorry, if I had examined your music more thoroughly I would have given you the different orchestra with two French horns; the medium orchestra."

"You mean—do over all that I've done?"

That gentle, kindly smile. "I don't think it would be so very much work. You might not have to do them all over, just substitute the instruments."

(Perhaps not for you, Dr. Jones. But for me, *the whole labor over*)

I could not do an orchestration at all unless I held the whole thing in mind from beginning to end all the time I was doing any part of it. And my carefree system of composition, the just "letting it come to me," had given me no practice, to date, in arduous intellectual musical concentration.

I had, in some way which I cannot explain, to find a center to it and feel its unity, the relation of every part to that center, and maintain this mental grasp until I had the whole score written.

And those words, "substitute the instruments," would never work for me. With two French horns in my orchestra that *center* would be quite different, I would have to find a new center. There would be melodies taken now by the horns that the cellos had taken before, changes in the clarinet part, in fact, in the whole thing!

No doubt, Dr. Jones, with a lifetime of drill behind him, did all this automatically, without effort. No doubt, also, he could sight read at a glance, and instantly know what each of the choirs was doing. Whereas my reading was slow and labored, I had to practically pick it out, instrument by instrument, then finally get them singing together in my head.

Of course I did not argue the point. I saw what he meant and felt myself that in the end the orchestrations would sound better.

But, Oh! the long weary hours of work—when there still remained so much to do!

Good practice for you, I told myself severely as I drove home.

Besides, I was thinking of the horns. They seemed like friends, there in the car with me. And I began to run through the musical numbers in my mind, recognizing many places where the horns would come in beautifully.

The way that long, cool, calm note floats—as a sea gull floats, I thought, high up there, alone, wings absolutely motionless, riding some current of air, a slow tilt and slide one way, then the other, and at last the big

[125]

swoop down to the sea. Yes, the horn rides. . . . floats on a current of harmony. . . . remaining motionless . . . . just a little tilt. . . . this way, then that. . . .

On the score you see the whole notes, just round empty circles, often held enharmonically from bar to bar, the long ties looping from note to note along the page.

And so I began the orchestrations again.

I felt a sense of pressure now that I never had before. So much to do over and so much still to do, and summer not far away when I would be in Tyrawley and Dr. Jones in Washington.

In addition Kent thought it would be a good time for me to dash off an orchestration of my piano étude, "Wind Harp." He had always loved that piece. How stunning it would be, orchestrated! Over there in Holland, he had now got acquainted with such a fine copyist; and he knew the conductors and orchestras; and just possibly he might get a performance by a good orchestra before he returned to the States!

I did not really think it wise. But one day, as I was waiting in the hall for Dr. Jones' door to open, leaning there in the window, looking down at the garden, I began to let the orchestra in my mind play "Wind Harp," and some lovely things began to happen; and I just couldn't resist it.

Before the cherry trees burst into bloom it was done, an arrangement with full orchestra. An immense piece of work.

Then heat descended on Washington. I packed my car with Hosannah helping. A box of books. Box of music. Tape recorder. Box of records. Box of orchestrations. Box of manuscripts. Book of themes. Twenty-two pieces in all besides my clothes, personal effects, and Persian cat.

I sped northward toward the cool green trees and the swimming pool at Tyrawley.

Fifteen

BEFORE LEAVING Washington I had discussed with Dr. Jones the advisability of my continuing to work with some teacher of orchestration during the summer. He approved, and suggested either the Yale Music Department, only a half hour's drive from me at New Haven, or Juilliard, in New York.

I knew that Yale was interested in no music that was not modern. I feared that Juilliard might be the same.

A letter to an important New York musician with whom I was acquainted brought a helpful answer. He had a friend, an excellent orchestrator, a pupil of Respighi (at this I got a shock). He would speak to him and arrange it. He enclosed the address and telephone number of Marco Frascati.

The Sam Fox Publishing Company had a sort of stake in my musical, as they were the publishers of the song, "Green Grass of Wyoming." They were always willing to let me have a practice room or office in their New York suite and now arranged that I could meet Mr. Frascati there. A grand piano, desk, and record player would be in the room and Mr. Fred Dooer would give me any help I needed and see to it that we were undisturbed.

At that first meeting Mr. Frascati and I sat opposite each other, just getting acquainted, lining up what we were to do; what, in fact, *could* be done?

A middle-aged, blond Italian, thick-set, impassive, bored. His English was fluent but carried such a strong Italian accent that he could have gone on the stage with it—*What you wanta?*

He thought at first that he was being engaged to orchestrate a musical, then that he was being engaged to finish orchestrating it. It took quite a long while for him to understand that I had done it, was going to continue doing it, was going to finish it; but wanted someone to help, to supervise, to look over my shoulder, correct, suggest—in a word, teach me.

This, one could see, simply disgusted him. I was going to have a big change now from Dr. Jones and Dr. Bernier.

There was one compensating fact: he did not like modern music. This was understandable since he had inherited directly from Respighi and Rimsky-Korsakov.

"How longa you study orchestration?"

"Two winters."

Shoulders, eyebrows, lips combined to produce a truly histrionic sneer.

"Orchestration is a life work. It is a great science. Who teacha you for these two years?"

I explained about C.U., the faculty, Dr. Jones.

"*Doctor* Jones? He iss a doctor?"

"A doctor of music. A professor."

"Oh! A professor! I don't think much of professors!"

I was eager to know of his own musical career, how he had learned, what he had done. It was an interesting story. He had been a child prodigy in Italy. His father had a band. At the age of eight, the boy had been the first trumpeter. Four or five years later he was at a Conservatory of Music, and the study with Respighi had come after that.

His entire life had been given to composing and orchestrating. The coming to America and settling in New York, had been for the better commercial advantages, but I don't think he liked America. Again (and often) I saw that slight lift of the shoulders, tilt of the head, the sneer.

He finally delivered his decision.

"I do not like teaching. It is very boring."

I inwardly agreed with him and was sorry it had to be inflicted upon him. But I needed him. This orchestration—I had my teeth in it and I would not let go. He went on doggedly.

"Besides, there is nothing in it." I kept silent. We had discussed the price per hour.

"But my friend ask me, and so. . . ." He did not finish, but again his shoulders went up in that expressive shrug.

So we arranged a date for an early meeting and I drove home on the Merritt Parkway, running over the musical numbers of *Oh! Wyoming!* Planning which ones to begin on.

First, I wanted to get his opinion on the orchestration of "Wind Harp." I had changed the last sixteen

[130]

measures since Dr. Jones had seen it and was unwilling to send it to Holland until these had been approved. Besides, I knew the general principles of the faculty of the Catholic University: never make things easy, make them hard. And there were pages covered with notes which, when I looked at them, gave me that sickening sensation of chaos.

I laid one page before Mr. Fascati and with my pencil pointed at a section: "What about this, Mr. Frascati?"

"Take it out."

"Why?"

"It's nothing at all."

"What about this part here?"

"Take it out."

"Why?"

"Just a conglomeration."

"And this part?"

"Take it out."

"Why?"

"It's a jumble."

"And this?"

"Take it out."

"Why?"

"It's a mess."

Why it should have been a relief to me to hear this is hard to understand, but it was, though it opened up terrible glimpses of other messes, jumbles, conglomerations.

The criticism suggested to me an orchestration freed of all the debris and beautiful as any created work would be—a house, a book, a piece of furniture—with its outlines clear, salient, and unencumbered.

At one swoop Frascati released me from the feeling that I had to keep all the instruments going all the time and I began to understand my besetting orchestral sin (which was taken right from my piano-playing methods); namely, allowing the orchestra to wander and improvise.

A little of this was pleasant and intriguing for the piano, but it wouldn't do for an orchestra.

Having eliminated the nothing-at-alls, Mr. Frascati wrote the word *solo* or *soli* over those instruments which had a telling bit of melody or rhythm to carry.

"It makes them play better," he said.

(I had read that Rimsky-Korsakov did the same. So here was Rimsky-Korsakov-Respighi-Frascati writing *solo* in my score.)

The process is similar to revising a book. Clarification. Enhancing all the merits. Eliminating ruthlessly all the negligible or bad.

I learned a lot.

The authorities and scores he quoted were Beethoven and Richard Strauss.

This gave me complete confidence in him, as did the fact that he sang all the parts—every instrument from double bass to flute going from one to the other; also acted them.

"Why you give the flute that horrible note?" (B flat) "Did you ever see a flautist trying to take such a note?" He slid from his chair, went to the center of the room, and became both flautist and flute, crouched over, the flute held to his lips, elbows pointed out and eyes almost popping from their sockets as he heaved and puffed, trying to hit that high B flat with the flute.

The same when I gave the double bass its lowest

note on the open E string. His impersonation of the double bass, with the right arm wielding the bow and deep growls coming from his vocal chords was something I'll never forget.

His favorite epithet was "horrible" or "monstrous."

The kneehole desk at which we worked was up against the left wall of the room.

It was *his* knees which were in the hole, and the score flat on the table under his face. My chair was drawn up behind his massive right shoulder which completely hid the score and anything he was doing with his right hand. I don't know how I was expected to see.

I sometimes stood up, and looked over. Of course, it is not very pleasant to have someone standing right over you, looking down practically on the top of your head; still it made me jump every time he commanded,

"Sit down!"

I sat down—fretted, worried, wondered, looked all around the room, at the pictures on the walls—finally stood up again.

And again, "Sit down!"

This more than doubled my work. I had to decipher all that he had done as soon as I got home: all those lines of notes which he had rubbed out (mine) and the other notes he had written in (his) and figure out *why* he had rubbed mine out, *why* he had written his in.

And then, invariably, I would find myself in a spot; for the last thing he would say to me as he handed me the page he had corrected was (with a contemptuous grunt), "Now you can send that to Holland."

But how could I send it to Holland when it was full of mistakes?

I would go back to him with the tale of his crimes.

"I had to change this, Mr. Frascati."

"What did you do to it?" (With a heavy frown.)

"Those measures for the English horn—you hadn't transposed them."

(He smoked heavily all through the lessons.) Now he took several puffs and nodded his head slowly. "You transposed them?"

"Yes."

"Good."

"And here are some measures without any accidentals; three are needed."

"You put them in?"

"Yes."

He nodded, puffed, grunted. "Good."

His writing was never free of mistakes. He showed definite annoyance when I made anything of it at all, assuring me, with his voice rising angrily, that in all orchestrations there were mistakes—always, always, always; it was in the rehearsals that these mistakes were worked out.

And I remembered Rimsky-Korsakov's despair over the number of mistakes, "swarms of them," so that for many rehearsals nothing could be done but locate and correct the mistakes.

Dr. Jones' umcompromising blue pencil would have been of help to both Rimsky-Korsakov and Frascati.

I had expected that a few hours of work on the "Wind Harp" would suffice and then we could begin on the musical; but he kept turning the pages in reverse until we were at the beginning, and here he leaned back and lit a cigar and looked at me.

"What is thissa? An orchestral piece with a piano in the orchestra, or a piano concerto with orchestral accompaniment?"

I could only stare at him. This question had never been raised before.

So we spent the entire summer on the "Wind Harp." I did not mind. It was knowledge I was after. I wanted to learn how to keep that sickening chaos out of my orchestrations. I wanted to know how to make those clear-cut little quartets and quintets of the woodwinds stand out with intriguing profiles, like cameos.

The two or three hour lessons two or three times a week were endurance tests for me—exhausting.

"The oboe is playing a solo? Keep the other instruments down, don't crowd him."

"But look at the pianist! Give him some help! The poor fellow is clawing at the piano with his bare hands!"

"Why you make-a the bass like thissa so often?" A savage stroke through it with his heavy pencil. "Put the accent where it belong—first beat in the bar, not last beat and then tied over."

"But I like it this way," I protested. "I don't like that mechanical *bang* in the bass on the first beat."

"It is customary."

But I continued doing it my way. He continued crossing it out, at last so massively that I could never again clean the spot with my eraser.

"Look Mr. Frascati, look at this place." I turned to a page where, after having withheld the bass note for six measures, I at last fell upon it with a deep boom—"See how wonderful it is here!"

"Well, that's just what I'm telling you."

[135]

"No. The point is, if I had used it in every one of those six bars I would have got no effect from it on the seventh."

He raised his eyes to look at me. He leaned back and puffed at his cigar, squinting at me through narrowed lids. I could see by his expression that he was going through that passage in his mind, first one way, then the other. At last he removed his cigar and gave in.

"You are the composer," he said seriously; and never again challenged that tied note in the bass.

There were pages in the score which I had altered on my own responsibility even though Dr. Jones and Dr. Bernier had approved them, changing sixteenth notes to eighth notes just because the passage looked so terrifyingly difficult for the strings to play; and it gave me considerable comfort and reassurance to discover that here Mr. Frascati found a good deal to praise.

In fact, he was as ready with "beautiful" as with "monstrous" when he felt it to be true, and it really thrilled me that he had the word in his vocabulary and was not afraid to use it.

"But not here!" he shouted. "See what the pianist is doing here! Take the orchestra off the poor fellow's back! Leave him alone!"

Frascati's contempt for "that professor" did not abate.

I had been dreading the moment when we would arrive at a certain page of the score.

When he did, there was an outburst. "That professor! I challenge him! Impossible! Absolutely impossible for the strings to play! Not even in *Die Valkyrie!* Not even in Strauss! And if they attempted it, what a mess! I bet that professor ten thousand dollars. . . ." and so on, while I listened, amused and entertained as when my stallion had put on a show, and wondering how long he could keep it up.

When he was pleased he made the same half-purring, half-moaning sound of pleasure Dr. Bernier used to make, almost always at some unexpected harmony: "Beautiful. . . . beautiful. . . ." nodding, singing, "Beautiful the way you have brought the cellos down here—but why did you not keep them down?"

"I was afraid the arpeggio in eighth notes would be too fast for them?"

"But why? Cellos can play like violins." and he began to sing the running cello accompaniment to the Michaela aria in *Carmen*.

I began to murmur the words, *"Je dis que rien ne m'e'pouvante. . . ."*

He broke off and stared at me, astonished.

"You know it?" he exclaimed.

It was after this lesson that he said, quietly and a little regretfully, "You will soon not need anyone to help you with your orchestrations."

Just occasionally it seemed to occur to him that he was perhaps being unnecessarily surly with me and he would give me a long and searching inspection. "It has indeed been a pleasure working with you."

My feeling about him was that he carried this spleen around—not because of anything that had to do with me. He was disappointed and soured by something; perhaps modern music; perhaps the fact that in America he could not find a musical world compatible to himself, to his past, to Respighi, to Rimsky-Korsakov.

[137]

When we came to the last lesson, if we had advanced from the next-to-last, when he spoke of the pleasure it had been to work with me, it should have been a love fest.

Anything but. We embarked on a tug-of-war.

It was all about what harmony the piece was to end on. He heard it one way, I another.

The ending of the piece was never amicably settled.

The ending of our summer-long association was just locked horns and a stiff good-by.

The orchestration was at last sent to Holland.

Sixteen

LETTERS FROM KENT during the last half year had kept me abreast of the work being done to prepare for performing and recording the six numbers of the musical which I had sent him.

When the cablegram reached me at Tyrawley, it was five in the afternoon:

> Performance and recording last night music
> terrific congratulations and love: Kent.

I rushed to the telephone. It would be ten in the evening over there.

Operator replied there was no answer.

But how could the house be empty? There were two little boys in the family, also housekeeper and housekeeper's daughter.

"There *must* be someone there, operator; please put the call through again."

"No answer, Madam."

"Then cancel the call."

Next day I tried again and this time got through to him.

I wanted to know if his word "terrific" was his own opinion or the conductor's. He gave an embarrassed little laugh but said nothing—which told me all. Well, I should have been prepared. I had often noticed, when listening to radio music coming from the northern European countries that they played nothing but the most extreme modern music.

"Did the conductor make any criticisms?" I asked.

"He did say you went a little bit heavy with the brass—drowned out the violins. . . ."

(My jazz orchestra, I thought bitterly.) I had never told Kent about Dr. Jones' change of my instruments, since there was nothing to be done about the orchestrations that had already gone to Holland, and it would only have worried him.

"Anything else?"

"Well, let's see. Yes, said it would have been easier if you had put the metronome time on."

"Which piece?"

" 'Midsummer Hums in the Meadows'."

"I'm sure I did. How did you like that piece?"

"Well, I liked it, but I must say it surprised me—it didn't sound like your genre at all."

"Any trouble with any of them?"

"Quite a lot of trouble with the Overture. They worked late on that, it was midnight when they finally recorded it."

"You were there?"

"Oh yes, from first to last."

Operator cut in. Kent raised his voice. "The records are on their way to you airmail!"

[140]

Rimsky-Korsakov, after having conducted an orchestra which was playing (or trying to play) one of his compositions for the first time, went home, put his head in his hands, and wept.

I didn't do exactly that when the records came, when I'd played it over once. I got as far as putting my head in my hands; then I began to laugh and couldn't stop.

I wouldn't have recognized my own children.

After a long while in which, when I stopped laughing, I just sat in that armchair with my mind a complete blank, staring out the window and watching the way the clouds crossed the sky, so slowly, I stood up and went to the Hi-Fi and said, Now let's see what's really wrong.

I played it over again several times.

One side of the record held the Overture and "Midsummer Hums in the Meadows." Both were impossible.

On the other side were the songs: "If Only," "Love at First Sight," "Early Morning," and "The Big Hill."

This side was really not so bad except that when, in "If Only," Joey begs Letty to give him just one kiss, the Dutchman sang passionately, "Choost one, Letty!" And in "Love at First Sight" the duet between Letty and her mother, they had chosen for the mother a contralto as ponderous as Schumann-Heinck's. "Early Morning" was all right. In fact it was good, Letty sailing up to her high C like a lark. But it was played too slowly.

As for "The Big Hill", this both infuriated and delighted me. When I had finished that orchestration Dr. Jones had said, "You have done this quite differently from the way it ordinarily would be done, but I think it may sound quite good." (High praise from Dr. Jones.) "Except that high B flat for the trumpet. You may not like that when you hear it, but don't change it. Wait until you hear it."

Well—now I had heard it and didn't like it. Nor did I like the way the orchestra dragged when there came the modulation from A flat to A natural.

What I did like was the four-bar period of drum beats. A familiar rhythm. In nursery days we used to march to it, beating drums or tin pans, yelling "Um pah pah, Um pah pah, Umpah Umpah Um pah pah!" This opened the march and occurred several times, unexpectedly, between the other periods. It made me laugh and I saw Dr. Bernier turn his head away with a repressed grin.

Listening to it now again I laughed again.

The Hi-Fi suddenly moaned to a stop. Something wrong with the current—this seemed the last straw. Well, I would try to get Kent on the telephone. But the telephone was dead. I tried the light switches—no lights.

I went out of doors and saw men standing where the avenue joins the road. A branch of the big maple had fallen, tearing down the electric lines. Live wires were writhing on the ground, smoking and sputtering. Repair men had been sent for; meanwhile police had blocked off the road and were standing on guard.

Next day I received a letter from Kent with a complete description of the whole performance and his own reactions. I think he must have been as upset as I at the first hearing, for he said, "I really didn't get it the first time. It was as if I just couldn't hear. Then suddenly it came through to me. Not the performance but the actual music of it—the way you sometimes have said of some artist's performance, 'He not only got it—he got the beauty of it.' That's the way it is with your music, not just music but the beauty that comes through it."

It comforted me, somewhat, that his final judgment had been more favorable. I kept experimenting with the records and found that in my first agitation I had improperly adjusted the volume indicators on the record player. Now the pieces sounded much better.

I talked to myself as one would to a disappointed child. Now you've got the worst behind you. Just cheer up and think of that! Nothing so bad as this can happen again. Slowly my emotion subsided and my critical faculties came to life. I realized that some of the music was awfully bad, some of it awfully good. Thank heaven for the good! What was bad should be eliminated—*must be.*

Before I went to bed that night I made plans. Go to New York tomorrow, to the Gotham Studios. Have them take those two numbers (the Overture and "Midsummer") off the tapes; make new discs of the others.

I have a book on lyric writing by Oscar Hammerstein with a preface by Richard Rodgers in which he says that to hear the music you have composed played by an orchestra is the best fun there is.

That was still ahead of me, yet not entirely. Now that I was accustomed to the slower tempos of the Dutch orchestra, I realized that one side of the record (with the songs) was really lovely. It gave me pleasure!

Before I fell asleep that night I thought of the eight dollars you pay for a seat at a Broadway musical. No wonder! The amount of toil and struggle and pain and disappointment and talent and virtuosity (as well as

money) to get just one good record of one good performance of one good piece.

When the tape had been corrected and the new
record made, eliminating the two failures, I tried it out
on everyone.

Peggy, at the opening of "If Only", where the two
clarinets go up in thirds, immediately smiled and said, "I
like your instruments."

Marion was enthusiastic and said she was going to
speak to a friend who knew a producer who might like to
hear it. His name was Lew Gosse. He owned a New York
theatre and had been one of the group behind *My Fair
Lady*.

Mr. Fred Dooer, who is in charge of orchestrations
at the Fox Publishing Company, heard it and immediately asked me who had made the orchestrations. When I
answered that I had, he almost glared at me.

"Are—you—kidding?"

Regarding my use of the woodwinds, Mr. Frascati
had given me several outright compliments, saying that
I made nice little quartets or quintets with them. In one
or two places he compared it to the way Strauss used
woodwinds. Dr. Jones had made similar comments.

Aroldo du Chène heard it and adjured me, "Don't
let anyone talk you out of the way you use your instruments."

"Which instruments?"

"I don't know exactly, but I think it's the wind. It's
quite different."

Presently I saw to my surprise, that Aroldo had
risen from his armchair and was marching up and down
the living room, his head cocked, his eyes glinting at me

and a crazy grin on his face. "The Big Hill" was on the Hi-Fi.

When the march was finished he exclaimed, "I wouldn't have thought it could be done!"

"What?"

"Another march! Totally different from all others! They're all pompous and bombastic but not this one. What's the name of it?"

"The Big Hill."

"Wrong title."

"I think it's an awfully good title for a march."

"But not this march! There's no struggle here, no big hill, no victory. This is just funny. And sophisticated. And very clever. Why, it's actually witty! Play it again."

I put it on again. He roared with laughter, "It's unique."

Mr. Freedman's office called asking if I had the recordings. Because two of the faculty of the University of Colorado were in town looking for a show.

I said Yes.

Miss Cohen, Mr. Freedman's assistant arranged an audition at Sam Fox Publishing Company. Mr. Fred Dooer officiated at the Hi-Fi, handling my record with possessive pride.

This was at the time, and has always remained in memory, a sort of dream experience. I had wakened that morning with one of the worst migraine headaches of my life—and as I have had a good many, that is saying something. I wondered if I would be able to drive down the Merritt Parkway, park my car, get to the Fox offices, carry through with greetings, introductions, explanations, talk, and so on.

There was another sufferer in the office.

Dr. Bell, the Musical Director of the University, was in excruciating pain due to arthritis, and was on his way to the doctor's.

I sat in a comfortable chair full of anacin and agony, listening—just floating away.

The room filled with men. Miss Cohen kept calling people and sending them in. I was vaguely aware that comments were favorable. Especially Dr. Bell's which came the last of all, just as he was struggling to his feet with the help of a heavy cane to go to the doctors. The other faculty member was studying the script, asking me questions.

Dr. Bell said briefly, "The music is a knock-out." and left the room.

His verdict thrilled and elated me. Another crack in the wall! He was, surely, intelligentsia. A doctor of music. Director at a university.

But their decision had to be "no". Their theatre did not have room for an orchestra, nor their stage for the scenes and cast of my play.

Jean Dalrymple called. She had a project to put several musicals on television. She was looking for plays. Would I consider letting her have *Oh! Wyoming?*

Knowing that, if I did, it would never be a stage play and that all the labor I had put in on it, arranging it for the theatre, would be lost, I said no.

"I don't blame you!" she exclaimed.

"You see, I've arranged it for the stage."

"I know! And it's a beautiful stage play, too."

When I told Mr. Freedman of this he seemed slightly outraged that she could even have dreamed of such a thing, and he said, "Why, if you had given it to her, do you know what you would have got for it?"

"No. What?"

"Ten thousand dollars. *And never anything more.*" (With an indignant look back over his shoulder as he left the taxicab.)

But—ten thousand dollars!

So. For what's there on paper today, I've been offered ten thousand dollars. There was some comfort in the thought.

The next telephone call was from Marion. Yes, Mr. Gosse would like to meet me, see my script, hear my music, and another little audition was arranged in Mr. Fox's office.

This time, no migraine. I was there waiting for him and enjoying myself at the piano, playing "Green Grass." A chorus joined in from the other side of the door. I grinned. It was the girls in the typing room—half a dozen or so of them. And when I stopped, they yelled, "Don't stop! Go right on!"

Mr. Gosse arrived. This proved one of the most interesting meetings I had.

We discussed the story, setting, he asked what the theme of the play was, and when I said it's contained in one of the lyrics, and recited it to him, his face slipped with pleasure and amusement. *When you get what you want you don't want it! When you want what you want, you don't get it! What you really do want, is to want, and to want! So go right on wanting. You've got it!*"

His amusement over this broke the ice and we chatted for a long time. He picked up the script again

[147]

and again, silently stood reading a page, then put it down and started pacing the floor. He said, "It has charm. It has quality."

The principle trouble: it was Americana. He told me everything Mr. Freedman had told me. *Oklahoma* could not be a success or even be produced at present. His group wanted something bawdy.

Then a frown tied his forehead in anxious knots and he said, "Yet—you never can tell—something like this might just sweep the country!"

He said, almost indignantly, about the music, "Your music is lovely. It is singable, it is melodious. Give a fellow that kind of music to sing and he'll really sing. Most of these composers are giving us such stuff that no matter how good a voice the actor has he simply can't sing it, because it's not singable!"

But, regretfully, the answer had to be "no". He wouldn't dare recommend to his group anything so special, so different.

All the trees in Connecticut were turning red and orange and gold. Under the apple trees the windfalls lay, perfuming the air with rich spiciness.

I packed my car for another Washington winter and did not forget to take the new record. I looked forward to playing it for Dr. Paul, Dr. Jones, and Dr. Bernier.

Seventeen

THERE IS NO CONCEIVABLE REASON why, at this point, I should have felt a pricking in my thumbs, but I did. As if there was enough force behind the show, or enough of a ground swell underneath it, to lift it and propel it forward. Toward what?

And when the telephone rang and the operator said, "Cheyenne, Wyoming, calling Miss Mary O'Hara," and I answered, and then heard Charlie Carey say "Is that you, Mary?"—I had a real hunch.

I was now in Washington, hard at work again with the new group of instruments.

The occasion of the call was that Charley had talked with the president of the University of Wyoming (at Laramie) about my musical. They had a big drama department, also music department, and a new theatre big enough for any cast, any play.

Moreover, Dr. Humphrey was at this very moment in Washington, D.C. and would like to call upon me to discuss putting on my show in the coming season.

I replaced the receiver and sat a few moments without moving. *This is it.* At last. No need for carrying a whole troupe including orchestra to Cheyenne which Kent had said would cost a fortune, or for the expenditure of other thousands of dollars for the rental of the Lincoln Theatre in Cheyenne, or the housing and feeding of our troupe for the week of the "Frontier Days" Rodeo.

In imagination I saw the large new theatre of the university (they do things in a lavish way in the west) and the large cast of my musical moving upon that stage, the college chorus and orchestra supplying the music, the college faculty—all, of course, doctors of music and of drama, highly educated and cultured men—having charge of everything.

I heaved a deep sigh and sat there for a while, feeling some of the burdens slipping from my shoulders.

This was what Mr. Freedman had been asking for. New York managers could fly out to Cheyenne to see the show there as easily as they could take a train from New York to Washington. (So I thought.)

Suddenly I was excited by the play itself, as if I had just seen it performed, and I seized the script and read it from the first to last page, laughing at the jokes, saying Oh! at the scenes of elemental grandeur.

I played my record over and over, hearing it, in fact, with Dr. Humphrey's ears and the ears of the faculty of the University of Wyoming.

Several of the faculty of the Catholic University had already heard it and, to my surprise, thought it pretty good.

When Dr. Jones heard "The Big Hill" (we were squeezed into the tiny cubicle off the library where the record-players were) he turned to me, holding his shoulders very straight and high, his eyeglasses only a few inches from my face, and exclaimed firmly, "Excellent!"

Not a word about that terrible modulation. Or about the way the orchestra dragged and couldn't get over the stile (I had thought it shamefully obvious). Or the unsatisfactory arrangement and alternation of the periods. Or the high B flat. . . .

"But that high B flat for the trumpet, Dr. Jones. It drags, didn't you notice? I'll have to take that out"

"That's the trumpeter's fault. Not yours. A good trumpeter could play that. He should have practiced it."

I wondered who was going to make them practice? and who would be the loser if they did not? I made a mental note to take it out.

I quaked inwardly when the Dutch baritone approached the point where he was going to plead, "Choost one, Letty." But no one seemed to notice.

Dr. Paul took exception to the heavy contralto in the Letty-Martha duet. As he is the one who conducts and coaches the Glee Club and all the choruses, this was particularly in his department. Dr. Bernier agreed with a slight shrug. True, the voice was too heavy, it did not go well with the soprano, still the duet went nicely and was, on the whole, enjoyable.

I spent a pleasant afternoon with Dr. Humphrey. He liked the project.

He held the script in his hands now and then glancing at it or reading a page or two. He explained that he would not, in any case, be the one to make the final decision. It would be Dr. Dunham of Drama, or Dr. Wilman of Music.

[151]

"And particularly Dr. Wilman," he said smiling. "When it comes to a musical it is always our musical director who makes the final decision."

He carried the script and record away with him and I remained with that name, Dr. Wilman, lingering in my ears. Wilman. . . . Wilman. . . . it rang a bell; where had I heard or read of Dr. Wilman.

It was some weeks later that I finally located it on page 295 of the autobiography of the French composer, Darius Milhaud.

It was during Milhaud's tour of the United States that he became friendly with Dr. Wilman, musical director at the University of Wyoming who organized a series of concerts of contemporary music to be sung by school children. Dr. Wilman assured Milhaud on a later visit that these children, so taught, had actually been able to sing the strange and difficult intervals of Milhaud's music.

What these intervals were I could imagine but, to refresh my memory, read over again, in Milhaud's autobiography, the chapter which describes the impression his compositions made when they were first performed in Paris. (Arnold Schönberg's hysterical Berlin audience surely had a rival here.)

". . . an indescribable tumult broke out, a real battle, in the course of which the organist had his face slapped . . . the din grew worse . . . the police intervened . . . balconies were cleared by the municipal guard . . . the critic thrown out by two policemen . . . noise covered the orchestra right to the end . . ."

If Dr. Wilman admired such a composer, how would my music—sweet and beautiful music—sound to him? I thought of the comment once made by Stravinsky to the effect that a major third made him want to vomit. Possibly at this very moment Dr. Wilman had my record on his Hi-Fi, was listening to those cantabile melodies in which occurred many a major third, many a perfect cadence.

A good deal of time elapsed. Letters came from Dr. Humphrey, pleasant, friendly, hopeful. Then silence.

I worked at my orchestrations.

At about Christmas time, when Kent was already writing me they were making plans for return to Washington in the spring, a package arrived from the University of Wyoming. Inside it were the script and the record.

An agreeable letter from Dr. Humphrey explained that, to his great regret, the plan had not proved feasible. It would have needed the services of the combined staffs of the drama and music departments. It would have consumed the best part of a year. Students came to the university to learn Shakespeare. . . .

In the spring a United States troopship brought Kent home; Kent and Deirdre and a new Mercedes-Benz car and Jonathan and Richard and a baby girl who lay on her back and specialized in contemplation of a foot raised vertically in the air—about as big as a mouse.

We all spent the summer at Tyrawley while Kent's Washington house was being vacated and made ready for him. During his sojourn at The Hague there had been opportunities for trips to London where Deirdre and he had bought, piece by piece, eighteenth century furniture paid for by the three-year rental of the Washington house.

When Kent's leave expired, they went to Washington and moved into the new house.

I followed later, wondering why the pricking in my thumbs continued. Perhaps it was mere determination, for I was feeling that, though a lot of preparation is always good, it was time something happened or began to happen.

I often wondered if Mr. Freedman had made many efforts to interest producers. Some people told me he simply waited for them to come to him.

But he had said he would talk to them and actually, what else could he do? If any had been interested, they would have asked to see a script. Perhaps he had shown the script. Perhaps not. I did not know. One got nothing out of Harold Freedman that he did not want to divulge, except, possibly a chronic pessimism. Yet I had a small but persistent hunch that he did have, somewhere in the hinterland of his thinking, definite hope for the show.

I was thrown back again on the possibility that C. U. might produce it. I sometimes met Father Hartke in the halls. We would pause and chat a moment. He continued to express the warmest good wishes for my project and particularly congratulated me on having Harold Freedman handling the play and using such an adulatory word as "superb" to describe the picnic scene in my second act. Then we would part pleasantly and pass on.

I wondered if the stumbling block could be my cantabile music. Dr. Bernier liked it. And I think Dr. Paul did too because he once told me he had been severely criticized for teaching nineteenth century music to his piano students. But how could you teach piano at all without Tchaikowsky and Liszt and Chopin!" he exclaimed.

How savage they are, these protagonists of modern music. Is it because they know they are standing with their backs to the wall that they dare to say, Nothing but modern music, or we will not let it pass?

At the university I heard more and more about the feud between the Drama and Music Departments. It was quite historic and had to do with the use of the physical plant itself. I finally concluded that it was this which blocked any possibility of their putting my show on.

I continued working at my orchestrations and helping Kent and Deirdre get settled in their new home. With a small baby to care for, Deirdre could do little running around that winter, so I ran around and was never seen without swatches of material or a small lamp or two under my arm.

Before going to Holland Kent had been indefatigable at "knocking on doors" as he put it. He now resumed this. On his fairly frequent business trips to New York he would take a day or two of leave and knock at doors of producers and managers—always to come up against one or more of those impenetrable *walls:* it's Americana, it's an original; it has no Names. It's not modern music.

He also visited play brokers. These were an important cog in the machinery of play-launching of which I had never heard before. They "handle" the plays, for a commission of course. There is Samual French for plays, also the Boston Play Company; Tams-Widmark for musicals, Music Theatre International; the Dramatists Play Service and a few others. Under certain conditions, specified in a contract, they take over a limited section of the market; then list the play in their catalogues and assume costs of publication, office work and promotion. This is the way a play is kept alive, produced again and again.

Frequently this brings the author royalties for many years. We are certainly still seeing not only Gilbert and Sullivan, but many of the successful Broadway shows as far back as one can remember. Occasionally such a company will share the gamble with a producer and tie up with a play before it is produced.

Kent found the heads of these companies to be men of high type, friendly, competent, willing to discuss matters and give sound advice.

He tried them all on *Oh! Wyoming!* One or two were doubtful, even said they would consider it, but nothing came of it.

Better than all the others he liked the Dramatists Play Service. This company charged only 20%, a comparatively low commission. It had been established by members of the Dramatists Guild of the Authors League of America (of which I am a member) for the handling of the nonprofessional acting rights of members' plays and the encouragement of the nonprofessional theatre.

Kent had some very good talks with Margaret Sherman, executive secretary, and Andrew Leslie, editor, who seemed favorably inclined but, as was the case with all the other companies, were afraid of tackling a musical. The difficulties of a musical were almost prohibitive.

Miss Sherman added that musicals, however, were in such demand that they might have to undertake them. But not yet. And in any case, they would take on nothing that had not been produced—though not necessarily on Broadway.

The Broadway opening gave these play brokers the magic words to launch their promotion campaigns: "Broadway," "Smash Hit".

[156]

But, by the same token, the rental that could then be charged to schools or universities would be high. Perhaps too high.

If it could be a musical that had been produced successfully (what did this mean? No actual breakdowns?) and which could be rented at a reasonable price then, possibly. . . .

Eighteen

DR. JONES' INTEREST in my work, as we proceeded with the orchestrations, continued to grow; also his conviction that this show was worthy of production.

He told me he thought it should open at some big festival, such as are held almost every summer in the south or west. I told him about the plan to have it go to Cheyenne, at the Lincoln Theatre, during the "Frontier Days" week, and he thought that would be ideal and wanted to know what was holding it up.

"Production," I answered and explained that I would have nothing to do with a careless, hastily thrown together show. It would have to be done here, by experts, and done with thoroughness, care, and skill. "And then the whole cast and staff and sets and props and orchestra transported out there."

It was obvious that the cost of all this would be prohibitive.

In spite of all these discouraging aspects, Dr. Bernier was a constant ally, quite sure that some day some way the production would come about and possibly at the Catholic University.

Now enters Matt Hillman, one of the "genius graduates" of Father Hartke's classes, at present instructor on the drama faculty. Matt had directed most of the operas and other productions performed by the music department.

It was Dr. Bernier who brought us together in midwinter of that year.

I had once, with amusement, told Dr. Bernier about the young lawyer who offered himself as my angel to the tune of a quarter million. He now wanted me to repeat this to Dr. Paul and Matt Hillman. We met in Dr. Paul's roomy office.

There is an undeniable power in such a figure: $250,000. And as, at Dr. Bernier's request, I quoted the exact words of the brief dialogue—

"What shall I tell my agent?"

"Tell him you've got an angel."

"How much of an angel?"

"How much do you need?"

"Perhaps a quarter of a million?"

"That's a snap!"

. . . a sudden deep silence settled upon the room. They all looked at me. I sat silent looking back at them. Waiting. Wondering.

It was Hillman who first emerged from the spell of that quarter million.

He is a handsome young fellow, Jewish, tall and dark. I say "young," but it is very difficult for me to estimate a person's age. If they are lively and alert and doing something interesting, they seem young to me. Matt may have been forty.

"If we should put the show on here how much of that could we draw on?" he asked.

"None of it," I answered; and explained the impossible condition attached; namely, that I myself should be the producer.

To my surprise this did not end the discussion. I got the feeling that in spite of Father Hartke's veto, the matter was still open. Hillman sounded me out as to whether I would be a rigid prima donna, refusing to consent to changes he might want.

"What changes do you want?" I asked.

"The Swedes," he answered, "in the picnic scene."

"What about them?"

"I want them out."

"Take them out."

He laughed. "You're too easy," he said.

Though this massacre was swift, I had flashed through the scene in my mind. It meant eliminating those parts of the picnic which were, possibly, what had made Freedman call it superb: the scene of the big bearded Swedes dragging the little dancing girls into the woods; the scene of the big men making their entrance by jumping from the top of the moving caboose onto the stage; also the various musical numbers that accompanied all this action: the Swedes' chorus, "Alas! Little Bird!" possibly the most moving and classical folk song in the entire show; the interlude which accompanied the change of light from afternoon to dark, "Twilight and Birdcalls" and the big dance, "Svenska."

"But why?" I asked. "Why do you want them out?"

He explained. "It's not that I don't like them, but there simply isn't room for them. The whole cast is already on stage. We wouldn't have room in the wings for another half dozen men."

Here was just the sort of thing I had anticipated. It applied, probably, to just this one stage. In a different theatre, the scene would be all right.

I decided to do nothing to the script until I saw whether anything would come of this conference.

Meanwhile, I timed the play with script, stop watch, clock, someone at the piano and someone reading dialogue and stage directions. I found that it ran, without intermission, for four hours—exactly twice too long.

I would have been glad to start the cutting immediately, particularly as I might at this very time be working with Dr. Jones on orchestrations of numbers which might eventually never be performed; but it seemed wiser to wait.

Nothing, however, came of that conference. I saw Matt from time to time as we came and went in the halls, he to his classes and I to my hours with Dr. Jones. Now and then we leaned together out of a sunny window, or sat on a garden wall, to ask and answer questions about the stage, plays, movies.

I gathered he had a violent and deeply rooted prejudice against all authors.

There is nearly always war between author and director. Sometimes a cold war, sometimes hot, occasionally very hot indeed. At any rate, chronic. If there could be close, friendly collaboration between them it would be ideal. I have experienced this once or twice.

There is reason for the antagonism. I must say I am sympathetic to the director. The material passes through his hands last. He has the final responsibility. He has to make it right, translate it from paper to stage convincingly and smoothly. *He* is responsible for the pace, for the acting, for meeting the deadlines. On him, mostly, will be heaped the blame or praise.

If I were in his shoes, I could not possibly direct a scene I disliked or disbelieved in. So my way with directors is to suit them if I possibly can; to alter, to yield, to rewrite.

Matt was frank about it. "I make a rule," he said, "if I put on a show, the author will receive two complimentary tickets. That is all he will have to do with it."

"That would suit me down to the ground," I said.

He felt it necessary to emphasize this still further. Looking me sternly in the eye: "I would simply refuse to do any show if the author had anything to do with the production!"

Surely, I thought, this is his roundabout way of preparing me for the news that they will make my play; but time went on, nothing more was said, and I concluded finally that though Dr. Paul and Dr. Bernier and even Matt might be favorably inclined, Father Hartke was immovable.

Nineteen

In June of that year, 1960, Kent and I decided to investigate the possibilities at other universities.

After all, only three had turned it down: The University of Colorado, University of Wyoming, and C. U.

In the environment of Washington there were three others. The Georgetown University, the American University, and University of Annandale.

Kent discovered the Georgetown U. had no facilities for such a show; that American U. did have and also the U. of Annandale. He also discovered that Dr. Yocum, head of the Drama Department of American, and Dr. Scott, Drama head of Annandale, were both graduate star pupils of Father Hartke's drama course at C.U.

The Catholic University, right where I was already installed, seemed the very ark of musical and dramatic erudition.

We discovered that both American and Annandale had scheduled a musical for production some time in the coming year and both were anxious to do an original if a suitable one could be found.

We submitted the script of *Oh! Wyoming!* Kent had conversations with both Dr. Yocum and Dr. Scott.

Dr. Yocum gave a prompt answer. He could not consider doing it. The play was far too elaborate, too long, too complicated. He did not feel certain that it could be cut to practical staging length without destroying some of the best effects. He added that it was very tempting, ". . . . an original by a famous author, then going out west during the week of 'Frontier Days' . . ." but altogether too large and risky an enterprise.

Annandale was also tempted but caught on a different snag.

Dr. Scott thought the script could be cut all right—he would help with that since there was no objection from the author. However, even when cut and simplified he did not think the play could be produced for the few (very few) thousand dollars which were allotted the Drama Department for its yearly musical. They could not attempt it unless Miss O'Hara would make a substantial contribution toward expenses. If he could be assured of that. . . . .

This was both good and bad. Encouraging, certainly —he must want the show. But what were we getting into?

We did not answer his letter immediately.

It was a piece of great good luck that brought Charlie Carey east at this time, to visit his married sister, for we were able to get together at dinner in the basement of my Georgetown house and talk over all the details, principally financial, of the Cheyenne performance.

Many things were made clear: just how the "Frontier Days" organization could help, and how they could not.

Charlie Carey would put us in touch with the theatre owner, Russell Berry; with a hotel manager to house our troupe; and best of all, would relieve us of all expenses of providing publicity for our show, because this would be bracketed with theirs. He told us the amount of money that would be spent on advertising their show (of course, an afternoon show) and promised that every dollar spent for them would be spent for us too (an evening show). We must understand that they would invest no money other than in the publicity. On the other hand, the take for the week's run of the show at the Lincoln Theatre would be entirely ours and this would be ample to cover the costs of transporting our troupe from Washington to Cheyenne.

This last was a bold prophecy. Neither Kent nor I could accept it as anything but counting a very big chicken before it was hatched.

But the atmosphere of our talks with Charlie Carey was warm and optimistic. Enthusiasm spread from one of us to the other and when he flew back to Cheyenne we were half committed in our minds. But before the show could be taken to Cheyenne it had to be produced in Washington.

I took another step forward. I wrote Dr. Scott that I would make a contribution toward the cost of production, the exact amount to be determined later.

Dr. Scott answered with an agreeable note, asking a date for a meeting at my house and suggested that we attend their early summer musical, opening in two days. He enclosed two tickets.

The musical they were putting on was *Pajama Game*.

Kent and I drove out to see it.

Dr. Scott had staged and directed it and young Ray

Hoffman, Annandale's musical director conducted it. The students performed it.

I thought it astonishingly good.

But the location of the theatre was depressing. It was in the outskirts of Washington, difficult to find; we twisted and turned through crowded, one-way streets.

And it was a small theatre; the audience was close to the stage. There seemed so few seats. I thought of my big cast! The windmill! The picnic!

If I was doubtful of the possibility of Annandale putting my show on, Dr. Scott was equally so. He talked to Kent and to me at various times, canvassing the possibilities. A good deal depended on what date would be chosen, for winter shows were subsidized by the university, summer shows were not. And yet it looked now as though it would have to be a summer show because of their crowded schedule. If a summer show— would it be possible to get a cast? Would amateur singers in sufficient numbers apply for auditions? "It is not likely that they would," he said, "though they might if we use your name to draw them in. Even so, the audience would be small and we could not run the show the usual two weeks . . . and it will be hot . . . we have planned to air-condition our theatre but that would hardly be completed in time. . . ."

It seemed, indeed, that the production was just melting away in perspiration.

Worst of all, I had no feeling that Dr. Scott had any enthusiasm for the play. He kept reassuring himself, as if talking to himself, muttering under his breath Father Hartke's four rules for a dependable drama.

It has to be moral. It is.

It has to build to a climax. It does.

It has to have a romance. It has.

It must have a sub-plot. It does have.

What he liked best of all about the play was the chorus of little milkmaids and the ridiculous notion that had taken possession of the owner of the dairy herd—that high milk production depended on the virtue of these girls.

How had I come by this nonsense? A bit of local fact. The owner of the highest producing herd of milch cows in Colorado would have nothing to do with milking machines or male milkers. Only female milkers. It was a short step in an author's mind to make the milkers little girls; the chorus. And another short step to premise that they must be good girls. Dr. Scott called it a delicious idea.

He laughed and his eyes lit up at the thought of the comedy scenes that would evolve out of this. One girl showing an empty milking pail to another, weeping at what would be thought of her!

I wondered uneasily how much length he wanted to give these scenes. They could almost run away with the show. I could imagine how the audience would guffaw. In my script they were just short bits put in to lighten other, more dramatic stuff. It was not, after all, a farce.

In all Dr. Scott said, he kept reminding me that Hoffman, not he, would have the final say. Everything depended on the music.

Hoffman was at present in possession of my score and orchestrations and was studying them. As soon as possible he would come to see me and talk it over.

I braced myself for that talk. Would he object because my music was not modern music? Or would that wall prove to have another crack in it, as at C. U. and U. of Colorado? (Dr. Bell: "The music is a knock-out!")

It did not. The wall was intact. And in no time at all, the battle line was drawn.

Twenty

WHEN RAY HOFFMAN CAME I was waiting for him down in the garden.

It was a hot night and it was pleasant rather than otherwise to see that he had no coat on: trousers dark and belted, a clean white shirt, simple dark tie.

He was trim and alert, of medium height, with thoughtful eyes behind his horn-rimmed glasses. I noticed his hands and forearms—brawny young forearms below the rolled up sleeves.

We went up to the music room and he unloaded the big book of the score, the script, records, and immediately delivered his verdict.

"It's dated," he said. "Why ever go back? This goes back to Victor Herbert. Why not go forward?" He placed his hand on the score. "If you could compose a score like this you could have done it the modern way just as well. Why didn't you? Did you think there would be a market for this kind of music? You must have thought so. I can't figure it out! It was a real shock to me to find that you had written this sort of derivative music."

[169]

"But everything derives. We derive ourselves. Music derives—and has to. Otherwise nothing has any roots or beginning."

"But then how can it have any originality?"

"Because *I* am original. *My* point of view—even though I'm writing about familiar things! I must just be true to myself. You don't arrive at originality by trying! That just makes you erratic, and forced, and peculiar. And that's the way most modern music sounds—done on purpose to be strange and different. Who wants that?"

I was launched on my favorite theme. I was certain, I told him, that if my music could only get past the musical intelligentsia—himself, for instance—it would find favor with the melody-starved, music-loving public. I had dozens of examples, quotations, remembered statements, including Rimsky-Korsakov's "Modern composers are so afraid to be commonplace they do not dare write a cantabile melody." And Rachmaninoff's: "The old music is of the heart, the new is of the brain." And James Stephens', "Originality does not consist in saying what no one has ever said before, but in saying exactly what you think yourself."

"Is there," I asked, "any tenderness in the new music? Any love?"

He turned his head away, repeating, "Tenderness? Love? Why shouldn't there be?"

"But is there?" I persisted.

After intense thought he put the question back to me very seriously, "Isn't there?" We cast our minds back over the musicals of the last years. And where we did find a few (those of Richard Rodgers and Frederick Loew) it was precisely here that they had fallen back into the traditional harmonies.

[170]

"And these were the popular songs," I reminded him. "When Rodgers wrote, for instance, the lovers' song in *The King and I* he was not "going back" to Victor Herbert, or any other melodist. And no more am I. I'm just writing the kind of melodies I like and that, to me, truly express those emotions which I am dramatizing."

Every so often he would say, doubtfully, "Of course you *may* be right."

He said once, "There are many lovely and wonderful things in your score."

"Oh, are there?"

"Yes."

"I'd like to know where?"

He sat at the piano and searched the score. He named the downward gallop at the beginning of "Green Grass" in the overture, and the way it came in again at the end. He named some of the development section of the "Wyoming Waltz." But it seemed to me he found very little he liked.

He spoke (really with disgust) of the preponderance of cantabile music.

I went to the piano and turned to "Don't Wish Him No Harm," a contrasting type. "Try that."

He played it and gave his verdict. "Positively operatic." He stood up and began to walk up and down the room. "What do you call this anyway? Opera? Light opera?"

"An operetta," I answered, "except that that word is no longer used. When it is really a play, with both dialogue and music it's just called a musical play."

"Of course that raises another question," he said, "Would it be possible for me to find a cast which could sing your arias?"

We went into that at length. When music is first composed it is impossible to know the range of the voices which will be taking the leading parts.

I said, "If the range turns out to be wrong for the singer, I will have to transpose or to change the melodic line."

"If composers would," he said, "but most of them won't."

"I would. I've given a high C to my soprano several times. I don't see anything difficult about that. When I was a girl I had an easy high C and many of my classmates had."

He nodded. "One year we had six sopranos with high C. This year, not one."

"If, when the play is cast, Letty cannot easily sing high C, she can sing one of the other notes of the chord, or the song can be transposed."

We turned the subject inside out. I found him very easy to talk to.

But we really got nowhere, except that I saw he was not in the least sold on the music.

"I don't see how you can make it," I said finally. "You have no confidence in it."

He put his hand on his heart. "That's it. No conviction."

"When I was a free lance scenario writer in Hollywood," I told him, "I made a reputation and a good deal of money just turning down offers. I would not, could not, and never did accept stories to adapt for the screen unless I had confidence in them."

Our eyes met. He grinned. I continued, "This means, in my opinion, you ought not to do this play."

He grimaced. "It's not as if we could just brush it off and say it stinks."

"Why not?"

"We *want* to do an original."

I laughed. "Many universities do."

"And Scott says," he continued, "that we're not likely to find anything better. It's got as good a story as any of them—a lot better than most. Besides, how can you tell in advance? Take *Pajama Game*—if that had been an original we would never have thought of doing it, the music isn't any good. Or *South Pacific* either."

"It must be hard for you" I said, a trifle sardonically, "to conduct music when it isn't any good. You'd be up against that with my show too."

He took a second to reverse himself. "It's not that I don't like it—much of it." He began to pace again.

"Oh, you do?"

"I play Chopin. I play Rachmaninoff!" He flung himself into the corner of the sofa. "But, you know, I have to justify the music to my orchestra."

I was surprised. "Your student orchestra? How do you mean?"

He went into a detailed explanation. "They say, 'but why do you choose such things as this to make us play? It isn't music. There are no melodies. . . .'"

"But you're pleading *my* cause!"

"And my first trumpet says, "I never have anything to do! I never play alone!"

I went to the piano and called him to look at certain parts in the score where there was a trumpet solo. "See here. . . ." I turned more pages, "And over here. . . . this obligato for the bassoon!"

His eyes flashed across the pages, took in those passages, exclaimed comically, "There you go again! Warbling!" and in an amusing but very true falsetto voice he warbled the cantabile passages, caricaturing them.

Next, I got a sample of Hoffman lecturing to his class on the history of music. I sat on the sofa and listened politely. How all this modern stuff grew out of Wagner's last work, from Liszt's last work; he touched on the difference between Beethoven's last work and his early work. All this was pretty boring since everyone knows it.

"All that's all right," I said. "I like variety. Much of the new music is splendid. I like to go forward too. But not to throw everything else out."

He burst out, "That first song, 'Green Grass,' really the theme song; why, it's like any hill-billy song!"

"That's what it ought to be like."

"Well, it's like a cowboy song!"

"But *it is!*" I exclaimed. "Don't you remember? The fellow who comes to the ranch singing it *is* a cowboy, isn't he?"

Hoffman went to the piano again and played "Green Grass." Sat silent, frowning at the music for a few moments, then turned pages.

"Remember, Mr. Hoffman," I said, "this is *popular* music. Supposed to be that. Supposed to be just light entertainment. Nothing highbrow about it."

"But it's not American music," he burst out. "You're American. Your books are American, but your music isn't. I don't feel it fits the locale. In lots of places you've written Viennese music."

"Only in the big waltz and bits taken out of it. There are three or four themes in it. The girl's song for instance, 'Early Morning'."

He played it. "Yes. This bit, this line here. Why should *you* write a *Viennese* waltz in an *American* play?

"Because in my young days I danced to it. Everyone did. In fact, the word waltz—it practically means Viennese. Certainly to all old-timers. It means 'The Blue Danube.' Out there, and in all the backwoods, they would dance the fast, whirling old-fashioned waltz. Even the old grandmothers get out of their chairs and begin to spin! You can write a new tune in three-four time and call it a waltz but it will never pull old-timers out onto the dance floor."

He stood up, thrust hands deep into his pockets, and frowned, silenced for a moment.

I went on. "And why do you pick on the Viennese particularly? There's also the Swedish folk songs. And the dance, 'Svenska'. And that Bolero—Spanish music."

"Yes, why?" he demanded. "Why Viennese and Swedish and Spanish?"

I put my hand on my breast. "Because they're in me. They are part of this country. In every kindergarten you will find little tots singing *'Sur le pont d'Avignon'* and *'Oh, du lieber Augustin'* "

"But you're American! You ought not to write music derived from somewhere else!"

"Aren't all Americans derived?"

"From Europe you mean?"

"Yes. Have you read Henry James?"

"Yes."

"Do you remember his saying that, as a writer living in America, he always had to refer to Europe to show his characters' derivations. So he moved to Europe."

"All Americans borrow then? And must borrow?"

"It's not borrowing. It's going down to their **own**

[175]

roots." I spoke with some heat. "Why should they repudiate that? But they do! Often the children refuse to speak the language of their immigrant parents!"

After a thoughtful silence he said in a low voice, "What do you think of parents who refuse to teach the old language to their children?"

"Where do your people come from? What would their language be?"

He turned his head away and looked down. "Polish . . ." and the connotations of this historic word thrilled me. Great wars. Great heroes. Great music. Chopin. Paderewski. "The Polonaise!"

". . . and Russian." he added. And I thought of those incredibly deep bass voices of the Russian choir singers rolling through their cathedrals like reverberating drums.

I thought of him and so many of his race (for Jewish means race to me, not religion) throwing away their heritage of melancholy and passion, of the long exile, of the world wanderings, of the endless race-suffering.

"And you want to throw all that away!" I exclaimed, "and write just an all-American musical!"

"Want *you* to," he corrected, smiling. "Feel you ought to."

"Derived from what?" I asked. "Wagner's last work? Or Beethoven's? To say nothing of Schöenberg's? Even if none of that is true to my own inner feelings?"

"Derived from American folk tunes. From Wyoming folk tunes."

"There aren't any. Buffalo herds, wild animals, red Indians—these don't make folk songs."

I thought of that big state, still half empty, just prairie lands, mountains, and semi-desert. Only in the

[176]

last hundred years or so have settlers come. Some were easterners, hunting for space and the frontier; but many were from the old country, and these brought their music and folklore with them.

"Listen," I said, "on my ranch the sheepherder was a Mexican. I had a Bohemian farmer; an Indian milker; and a Swedish foreman. They all sang and whistled what they had heard all their lives, or over the radio—bits of opera, European folk tunes, drug-store cowboy songs."

He listened, and considered all I was saying. Now and then he said doubtfully, "You *may* be right."

The evening was passing and we did not seem to be approaching agreement. I asked him, finally, to be a little more explicit. The score, as I had written it, was what we had to start from. If he simply could not accept the genre of my music, there was no use in talking further. But was it possible that, without actual mutilation, it could be modified to bring it into line with what he would approve of?

He sat down at the piano and got to work on the Overture. I then listened to some interesting sounds. It takes great skill to do what he was doing: an extemporaneous rearrangement which took the clear outlines of melody and phrases out of the music, telescoping it all together, turning it into a confusing jumble. I began to recognize the nervousness and haste of modern stage music. The singable quality was disappearing out of it, the "warbling", the cantabile melodies and cadences. And I remembered that producer, Lew Gosse, who had said so indignantly, "the music composers are giving us today, could not be sung by anyone—no matter how fine the voice." My score was becoming unsingable.

[177]

I wondered, I really marveled at how anyone can think that is what audiences want.

When he came to the finale and played the first measure or two he stopped and said, "This is good." Played a little more, stopped, and said, "But you've marked it *largamente*. Do you really mean that?"

"Try it the way you'd like it."

He played it fast—and all impressiveness was gone.

He continued to rearrange and I to listen, feeling more and more certain that we would find no middle ground to meet on.

I asked him how he liked the story. He didn't like it.

"Well—you don't like the story, don't like the music, I don't see why you are considering it at all!"

"Will we ever get anything better?" he argued. "And we *want to do an original!*"

"What do you dislike about the story?"

He thought Martha's protest at her daughter marrying a "lost boy, without family, home or name," would be suitable to a Boston Grand Dame but not a backwoods housewife. That Hank's bribe of a sheep dog puppy to the Mexican was hardly adult in these days when we expect to see knife-throwing and killings on stage. And there was philosophy in the play—which is out of place in a musical comedy.

"Yes, that's it," he said finally. "The play's *reflective!* That's what's the matter with it. And your music is reflective too."

As we went down to the garden, we talked about the orchestrations. He thought they were "not bad."

"You've worked with Dr. Jones," he said, "and he's a wonderful craftsman, has had no end of experience. But

[178]

they ought to be done over by a Broadway man, someone like Charley Cliff. He could give them brillance."

At this thought he brightened up. "It may be that is all that's needed," he said.

It was after one a.m. We stood at the gate a few moments and he said more than once "Well, I think it might be worked out. . . ." while I was thinking just the opposite.

We shook hands and I said, smiling, "I believe this play will be a success. And shall I tell you why?"

"Yes! Tell me!"

"Because of the music!" He laughed.

"You *may* be right."

As I walked slowly back through the garden I mulled it over.

An astounding phenomenon, I thought, that, contrary to the tastes and desires of millions of music lovers, a handful of musical sophisticates decided on the future of music, were able to create a vogue, and united in a conspiracy to condemn and obliterate all compositions that were contrary to their decision. So that Juilliard could announce over radio, "If Haydn or Schubert were composing today they wouldn't even get a hearing."

It was as if the issue had been taken to court and a verdict rendered by an omniscient authority.

Who is this musical dictator? And why do the critics obey so slavishly, one after the other handing out the stereotyped notices: "derivative, obvious, sentimental?" The words are loaded with bias and are not even accurate in many cases. They *could* say, "This music is melodious, has familiar harmonies, and is infused with warmth and feeling."

But no. Such words as those might draw in a big audience to hear the kind of music which is enjoyed. Such words would not deliver a death blow.

And again I remembered Adolf's sentence: "We will not let them pass."

As I went into the house I was protesting, "But why, Adolf?"

I closed the door, went about locking up, and Adolf was answering me.

"There has to be mass production of music today; we need so much—movies, radio, TV. And there isn't enough inspiration to go around so we do it with machines."

"Machines?"

"Brains. Ratiocinations. And then we protect it with a kind of a ten commandments. A lot of thou shalt nots."

"And the first is: nothing pleasant; nothing flowing and graceful and curved as so much is in nature."

"Well, yes—in a way. But we call it something different. We say, no sentimentality."

"Ah!"

"There was a little slip there. We got off the track at the very beginning."

"How?"

"Really the fault of that word sentimentality and its differing definitions. Many people recognize no difference between sentimentality and sentiment. So both are ruled out."

"And what *is* the difference?"

"Sentimentality is sob stuff. A pretence of emotion; exaggerated, false, immature, and unrealistic."

"And sentiment?"

"Is the real thing. Feeling. Without which any artistic creation is dry as dust and cold as death."

I lay awake for hours that night, seeking that dividing line between sentimentality and sentiment. *Feeling.* Is there anything more universal? Pass a friend on the street—the flashing warmth of the smile and glance and handclasp; or see the color fade from a face under the impact of sudden dread; or hear a voice that is suddenly bursting with longing; and longing is so often nostalgia.

"Why, Adolf, emotion is everywhere. It is life itself!"

But Adolf answered me no more.

Twenty-One

NEITHER KENT NOR I felt any jubilation. Yet it looked as though, doubtful, uncertain, dismayed as we were, still we were staggering toward a production at a university which was hard to find, lost among the winding roads of the suburbs, on an unseasonable date, in sweltering heat, with a producer who would do the show because he could find nothing better.

I received a letter from Dr. Scott in answer to mine. He regretted to say it was going to cost more than he had thought. Technical direction, construction costs, lighting, costumes, a flat fee for Ray Hoffman, "and in addition to a fee to cover extra rehearsals *as there will be many changes.*"

I could guess what those changes would be. Changes to eliminate any "warbling".

I wondered if Hoffman was counting on forcing me, once we got into production? Wondered if I was walking into battle? If so, with whom, Hoffman or the new orchestrator, Charley Cliff? Possibly both?

I decided finally that I had been underestimating this young man's strength of determination. And perhaps he had been underestimating mine.

Cease warbling? No, I would not. "Mary's tunes." These had been dedicated to this very musical since I was a child. And was not the word melody written on my banner?

Dr. Scott's letter ended with the sentence, "I was thinking in terms of twelve or fifteen hundred dollars, but I fear it will be twice or three times that much. I am sorry to discourage you. Please let me hear from you."

After some delay I wrote Dr. Scott: "Thank you for your letter. I am sorry I have not been able to answer sooner. Kent and I have been thinking it over. You will want to know which points present difficulties. The most serious is the summer production with heat, small attendance, and doubt of getting a suitable cast. Also formidable is the cost. I thank you most sincerely for the time and thought you have given this. The discussions with you and Ray Hoffman were stimulating and I know we could work well together. You may hear from me again. May we leave it at that for the present? With kindest regards. . . ."

I was, of course, still working with Dr. Jones and told him about the prospect of an Annandale University production. He was pleased and interested. He knew Charley Cliff well, he had once been a student at C.U. He told me I could not do better than engage him to do those orchestrations for which I would not have time. "He is one of us."

I wondered if Ray Hoffman was counting on Charley Cliff to telescope the score as he had telescoped my overture? Or would he do that himself? Professional orchestrators do not as a rule change the basic musical material. It is simply not done. Would Cliff prove an exception to this rule? And if he would and could, was I going to allow it? There were degrees, of course. I might shorten it somewhat, condense somewhat, eliminate some cadences and stops and starts, play it all faster and louder, but not eliminate the cantabile, no never. Nor my nostalgic harmonies.

I complained to Kent: "What a pity it is not C.U. They like my melodies there. I wonder if I should try Father Hartke just one last time?"

"He's turned you down again and again."

But I had never offered C.U. the deal I was offering Annandale now.

The more we thought about this the more illogical and unfair it seemed. Before parting from Catholic University I must, we decided, let them know exactly what assistance I was ready to give a production. I must offer it to Father Hartke one last time; and Dr. Jones and Dr. Paul and Dr. Bernier must know too. For the record, it must be in writing. A letter, I thought; a letter to Father Hartke, but unsealed and enclosed in a covering letter to Dr. Jones which would explain how this had come about and ask him either to forward the enclosed letter to Father Hartke, or to acquaint him verbally with the contents.

Dear Father Hartke:

In the continuing evolution of my play, certain things have happened which make me hope that you might be interested in producing it next May or June.

First: it can have a week's engagement at the Lincoln Theatre, Cheyenne, July, 1961.

Second: I have an angel of modest dimensions who will see to it that a university production is not handicapped by the lack of a few thousand dollars and that the troupe can be transported to Cheyenne after the Washington opening.

Third: a shortened and simplified script.

Fourth: a year to prepare.

University of Annandale is interested in producing the play under these conditions, and this letter is just to let you know about it before I come to an agreement with them.

With kindest regards.

Father Hartke said no.

As Dr. Jones conveyed this not unexpected news to me over the telephone, I quickly began to say my thank-you's to him for he had taken the trouble to talk to Father Hartke personally about it. Then I realized that he had more to say.

"But there is something else, Miss O'Hara, which might offer a possibility."

I again thrust the receiver against my head, all my hopes rising.

Though the Drama Department had refused, he said, there was still the Music Department. The rule of the university was that they helped each other. If Drama made it, Music would help and the run would be two weeks. If Music made it, Drama would help; and the run would be three or four days.

The spot for a musical next spring or summer was still open. If I would be satisfied with the three or four day run and fulfill all the other conditions I had mentioned in my letter, the Music Department would make it.

"Yes, Dr. Jones, I would be satisfied . . . yes, all the other conditions would be fulfilled as stated in my letter . . . yes . . . and yes . . . and yes . . ."

I had no sooner hung up the receiver than the bell rang again, and then again, and again . . . Dr. Bernier congratulating me, and then Dr. Paul and then Matt.

So easily—so simply the big things come about. As if they had been there waiting all the time; as if only a few cobwebs have to be brushed aside before they can be plainly seen.

Tracing events back, as I always like to do, I reached Dr. Bernier and the yellow pages; and before that, Flicka and Hollywood. Yes, it was all Flicka I saw. Flicka that had made my name so prominent in Wyoming that such a plan as this could be taken up and promoted with such enthusiasm out there. Flicka that made each of these universities interested in doing a story by me. Flicka that had sold enough and more than enough copies to bring in the costs of putting this show on in the east and transporting it west. Flicka. All those millions of copies that were now piled like a mountain behind me, exerting such pressure that one could almost feel them pushing. . . . But when one traces events back, where does one stop? Past, present, and future: are they all one? One immense screen on which the pictures parade endlessly?

Measured by the calendar it had been five years of work.

Suffering? Yes, some. Some blows, by their very nature, are fated to reach their mark. There is nothing to do but receive the hurt, absorb it, and go on.

As when Kent brought the word from California that "merit has nothing to do with it."

As when I learned that by doing it all myself I had possibly doomed it.

Again when Dr. Jones told me we must change to a different orchestra.

There was also the suffering I had experienced in my struggles to master the science of orchestration, or rather, when I realized that it was not possible for me to do so. This still grieves me. It will be my sorrow till I die. For I love the orchestra. It is my own true instrument.

The great satisfaction was to find that the wall which barred out all melodious music did, after all, have a crack in it.

Twenty-Two

THERE WOULD BE no possibility of my going to Tyrawley this summer.

At the university, although we had a year to prepare, there was a quickening of pace.

It was important to find our technical director (designer) early on. I was anxious on the score of my difficult "gimmicks," and made one condition to Dr. Paul: that he must be a man of mature judgment and ample experience. I wanted no youthful experimenting.

Dr. Paul agreed and said that he would get James Waring, veteran of half a lifetime's experience, a designer on whom Father Hartke as well as he himself could always rely.

Mr. Waring read the script and reacted disappointingly. He was afraid he would not have time to work the job in with his other commitments. A tactful "no."

Dr. Paul felt sure he could persuade him, given time. And went on with other business.

The "angel of modest dimensions" of my letter to Father Hartke evolved into a small company, the Markane Co., Inc., to sign checks, keep accounts, and be announced to the public as producer of *Oh! Wyoming!* in association with the Catholic University Music Department.

This brought a firm of Washington attorneys-at-law into our line-up and took considerable time.

A production manager was engaged, Vincent Walter, a genial young man, another brilliant graduate of the music school.

Dr. Paul, his assistant Mike Cordovana, and Vincent Walter began investigating methods of transporting the whole troupe to Wyoming. Should it be by chartered bus? Airplane? Train? And what firm of moving-vans for sets and properties?

Complicated insurance for personnel, accidents, properties.

Publicity was planned; tickets were printed and the sale of them, both in Wyoming and in Washington, arranged, not forgetting accountings for income tax. Artists from the C. U. Art Department were started on sketches for fliers and posters.

Applications for the job of designer reached my desk together with sample sketches. The name of William O'Donnell signed the sketches.

I asked how old he was and how many musicals he had designed.

He was twenty-two and this would be his first musical.

I said no, and sent his sketches back.

The other designer under consideration, James Waring, had not yet consented, Dr. Paul told me; but he was still sure that he would. I tried to see Mr. Waring myself, but he vanished and became incommunicado.

The immediate job which faced me was the cutting of the script. Matt, fortunately, had forgiven his author for being an author. I was thankful that we had had a chance to become friends. With his help and my willingness to slash where slashing was necessary, it ought to go quickly.

But Matt said, "Oh, no." (with a big grin) "It's your baby. You cut it."

I could not believe he meant it and tried him again and again and found out how expert he was at eluding and evading. He simply would not. I looked around for help and met expressions that were blank or meaninglessly diplomatic.

Not surprising. How would anyone dare to take such a responsibility?

But I longed for a consultant. In Hollywood there had been one dramatist. I helped him, and he, me. In such a difficulty, a meeting of perhaps three minutes, a few words, and then the finger laid on the page—this could go out, and this, and this.

Here in Washington. . . . mentally I searched the face of everyone I knew. There was no one who had that sort of knowledge, except, of course, Father Hartke, so I shut myself in with the script and watch and metronome.

There is that old saw: a play is not written, it is rewritten.

I had already rewritten mine many times, but it had not yet found its true, final, perfect shape.

A play grows, stretches, expands; then pauses, trembling and vibrating uncertainly; then slowly begins to contract and solidify. Finally, trimmed down to absolute essentials, it crystallizes. It has found its shape.

It is the same with movies, short stories, novels. It is only those who know very little about writing who expect a work to reveal all its best possibilities the first time it is tried.

Matt's refusal is easier for me to understand now than it was then.

What happened so easily with me—that my whole and my best and most concentrated attention was triggered when I worked on the script—only happened with him when he worked on stage.

He was behaving as though there would be plenty of time to do anything he wanted to the play when he got into rehearsals.

So I had to realize that even when I had cut the script it would not be final, it would still have to be put to the test. It would still be just theory, in the blueprint stage.

Architects say that plans and specifications for a house are nearly always changed during the building. And even in placing furniture in a prearranged pattern there will be changes: "No, no, that looks clumsy! Try it here! No, it crowds the sofa, try it there. Or under that window? Ah! that's it!"

Like the story of the three bears. The first bed too large, the next too small, the third just right. And the porridge: first too hot, the next bowl too cold, then just right.

Three times. I groaned. Did this mean three try-outs?

One reads in the newspapers the terrible stories about plays destined for New York when drastic, last-minute changes are made; whole chunks thrown out, cast or director changed at the eleventh hour; actors rehearsing the new arrangement all day long, appearing in the old every evening; author, composer, copyists, designer, director, and stagehands working without sleep or pause, dead on their feet, keeping going on coffee, on benzedrine; while the play and all its machinery staggers from one try-out to the next, from Washington to Philadelphia, to Boston, to New Haven, and so at last to Broadway.

And if it is a musical, for every page of script that is changed there are about four of music, original autograph, piano-vocal, orchestral score, extracted parts—all of them first copied by professional copyists, then printed. A major operation.

The marvel is that any survive. One columnist asked how it was that anyone thought it possible to rearrange orchestral music in a hurry since the great masters took years to do it?

A revue, I thought, might come through without damage, for each scene is judged for itself. But in a story, in a well-constructed drama with climaxes carefully placed and build-ups timed to a half-minute, the process might be fatal.

Of course, it is the author who has to do it, I thought, and practically alone. And if a number of people did try to do it together, they would not agree; every person would want to leave out something different and in the end they'd have nothing. I had seen this happen in Hollywood.

So I took knife in hand.

The play ran four hours. It had to be cut to two.

What was it going to be like? This is the great danger of an original. No one has ever seen its true shape.

With doubt and compunction, fearing that I was robbing the play of an immense theatrical effect, I cut the locomotive. And then the caboose, the Swedes, the storm, the rainbows, the scene of light changing from day to dark, the rhythm band made up of the Mexican's small children.

Of the music, this took out "Alas! Little Bird!" "Svenska," "Midsummer Hums in the Meadows," "Twilight and Birdcalls," and the scenic music "Storm," "Rainbows," "Windmill."

It now ran seven minutes short. I wondered if this mattered. If it was not actually a good thing. Production Manager Walter disabused me. "That is the worst thing that could happen—as if we didn't have enough material really to make a full length show."

I put back the storm and rainbows with great relief. No one, at any time, had suggested leaving these out. I think we all felt that such unusual scenes, together with the (quite wonderful) storm music, would lift the play above the average.

"These scenes," someone said (I am quoting a remark made a few months later), "are going to make theatrical history. . . ."

". . . people will simply run screaming out into the streets. . . ."

In the fall, when all the students had reassembled, we cast the play.

In Dr. Scott's letter to me he had expressed fears that, if the show was to be put on in the summer, few amateurs would present themselves for auditions.

There was no such difficulty at C.U.

During an academic year, Dr. Paul frequently makes

[193]

trips to various parts of the country to audition singers, as
well as pianists and instrumentalists, for admission to the
music department.

Arriving at airports, met by educational or political
dignitaries (and the Press) Dr. Paul's impressive appearance was an immense asset. Tall, well-set-up, energetic,
he had a direct gaze from behind owlish, black-rimmed
glasses. He said little, listened attentively, seldom smiled.
His bland expression left you guessing.

Such vocal students as had fought their way up
through school competitions until they had won top
awards, sang for him. He offered the best of them scholar-
ships to Catholic University, and so brought them to
Washington.

We sat at the table in the big instrument-clinic room
upstairs; Kent, Matt, Vincent, Dr. Paul and I; and listened to a group of singers that would have delighted the
ears of Rudolf Bing.

A fifteen or sixteen year old blond tried out for the
star part of Letty.

The word "blond" calls up a vision of honey-
colored hair with silken sheen rolling upon the shoulders. But not this girl. Her hair, upon which had been
perpetrated some sort of permanent wave, was in a color-
less and shapeless bush around her head. "Blond" means
only that the thick fuzz which covered her bare knees was
very light; the knees, knobby and innocent, rose out of a
pair of rubber boots.

When she opened her mouth—the sweet unpainted
mouth of a child—and sang, one forgot the short out-
grown skirt, the ungainly jacket (it must surely have belonged to an older brother) and heard only so pure and

[194]

full and rich a tone, combined with a musician's skill in using it, that we, sitting at the judge's table, looked at one another and smiled.

There followed a dramatic soprano who made me think of the winter I spent in a boarding school in Italy. The Italian peasant, rather squat and heavy, always dressed in black, often had features so beautiful one remembered ancient Greece.

Here she was, standing by the grand piano, dressed in plain black cotton, pouring forth glorious sounds, but with total immobility, almost woodenness, of expression.

There were perhaps half a dozen sopranos who could have sung Letty's part, with all its difficulties, its bold high C's—and without the slightest trouble.

But Dr. Paul had already chosen our Letty. Marilyn Landers. In addition to the easy high C's, and a voice to do anything she wanted, she had a quick and graceful body with a small waist you could clasp in your two hands, a face of sweetness and beauty, and also the star quality. I don't know what it is. But when she walked on stage, she took the stage.

She had a voice equal to anything I have ever heard on Broadway, unless one goes back to Calvé.

She had sung many leading parts in off-Broadway shows, summer stock, amateur productions. She had come, now, to C. U. for coaching from Dr. Paul's assistant, Michael Cordovana, and his vocal instructor, Raymond McGuire.

I asked her one day if she liked her songs. After a moment's hesitation, she put her hand on mine and said, "I think you fell so in love with Joey Bud you gave him all the best songs."

[195]

That was a surprise to me. Of course, it was a male lead—Joey had more singing to do—but only a little more; they had three or four big duets together. I registered a determination, right then, to build up her part, especially her songs. An audience is always partial to the leading lady.

Dr. Paul had already told me he thought Jimmie Gilleran, who had graduated from the music department the previous year, would be the one to play Joey. He was in the Army chorus and was tall enough, slim, handsome. I looked at his pictures and said, "But he's a comedian."

Dr. Paul assented. I did not want a comedian for Joey.

But when, at the audition, Jimmie stood up and gave his music to the accompanist I saw that as a comedian he was miscast. He was in uniform, erect, with shining buttons, trim hair. In a straight role he could hardly be bettered.

His voice rolled out easy, warm, a trifle sad. I thought of the singing climax and his lines:

I'm like the tumbleweed—that prairie bum,
See 'em go blowin' and boundin' over the rollin' plain!
    Travelin' miles and miles—roots in the air,
Always a-movin' on—goin' nowhere!

We, at the judge's table, scribbled on our cards. It was unanimous. Jimmie was Joey. He was actually romantic! What luck for the show!

We had no difficulty in finding a Martha, a Hank, a Nicki, and a Jepson Heath. But not Windy. We had known he would be hard to find.

Months went by. There were some fine bass voices in the C. U. faculty, but not one could go to Wyoming in the summer.

Dr. Paul got too nervous to wait longer and at last called a repertory theatre and bought a fine bass voice, John Miller. Markane Company signed a pretty big check.

Copies of the new shortened script were made and distributed. The players began to learn their parts and rehearsals were begun.

Twenty-Three

WE HAD NOT as yet decided on our technical director.

When I asked Dr. Paul about Mr. Waring he seemed troubled and could only repeat what he had said before; that Waring would never let him down; that if no other designer were found, Waring would work the job in somehow, no matter how busy he was with other commitments.

This troubled me too. Greatly. I didn't think the scenic effects of *Oh! Wyoming!* were going to be very easy to "work in" anywhere.

For some time now a big young fellow with dark hair and a round baby face had been hanging around the halls. I passed him once or twice near Dr. Paul's door and noticed how smart and well-dressed he was in comparison to other undergraduates. I wondered who he was.

One day there appeared on Dr. Paul's desk a tiny model of a windmill. Standing behind it, like a puppeteer manipulating his puppets, was the same young man in a handsome camels-hair polo coat. He made the windmill rise magically out of the earth and sink back in again— up and down, up and down, as easily as a fountain rising and falling. The trick was done by invisible threads, attached to two rings, the two rings for the young man's two forefingers.

This was Bill O'Donnell who, two years before, had graduated from the Catholic University's Drama Department, hailed as another of those geniuses. He went from C. U. to the department of scenic design at the Metropolitan Opera House in New York and had been working there on their technical crew ever since.

Dr. Paul sent for me. I saw the windmill. I saw Dr. Paul's pleading face. "Such a relief," he said, "after all the discouragements, the worries, to see such enthusiasm—."

"Enthusiasm?" I asked.

"About your play," said the diplomat.

"Oh! He's enthusiastic?"

"He's simply crazy about it."

I realized Dr. Paul had practically given up hope of getting Mr. Waring.

Bill O'Donnell was engaged.

None of my forebodings left me. If anything, they increased, especially after my first good long talk with Bill, his "enthusiasm" simply terrifying me. I am sure, if a scene had called for a cow to jump over the moon, he would have obliged. Where an experienced designer would have persuaded me to delete certain of my scenes as too costly or even impossible, Bill would exclaim, "Over my dead body!"

He it was who said that theatrical history would be made by this play. Who said, "They'll run screaming out into the streets!"

He it was who informed me gleefully that my first script had twenty-seven scenes. "Did you know, Miss

[199]

O'Hara? And there isn't a page of your writing that doesn't have scenic effects in it that would drive any designer mad."

He it was who had been sending sketches and applications for months. "I was simply determined to get on this play!"

"How did you dare?" I asked. "With a script that had twenty-seven scenes?"

"Oh! I thought it would be exciting!"

"What about the storm? The lightning and rainbows?"

"I know just how to do it. Lightning is of all different shapes. I've spent hours at the Metropolitan Museum in New York getting pictures of different kinds of lightning."

There was something else that worried me. Not only Bill, but all these young people who had grown up in the large eastern cities, seemed abysmally ignorant of farm life, of domestic animals, of the countryside itself. They did not know whether a cow's tail stood up when it was being milked, or hung down; or, really, which end it was milked from. Bill did not know. He thought the tail stood up and so painted it (without asking me). He backed the hind ends of the cows into the mangers against the feed boxes and so had them painted (without asking me).

(Shrieks from the audience greeted this milking scene, especially in Wyoming, while I sat with nails dug into the palms of my hands; but the scene was always a success. I think the audience accepted it as intended comedy. It certainly was funny.)

But there were other things Bill did know.

Every graduate of Father Hartke's drama school was

supposed to be an all-round theatrical expert: play-wright, designer, stage manager, director, actor; eventually the natural talent of each emerged and predominated. Matt, I was to find, was primarily actor. Bill, to my surprise, understood play construction.

As rehearsals progressed there was general agreement that there was a drag in the second act. It just slowed up. Something wrong with the script?

"What do *you* think?" And it was Bill I was talking to. "Do you see anything unnecessary?"

"I hate to admit it, because I love the scene." Bill put his head sadly on one side. "But it's the owl-leotard scene. I've been looking forward to designing it, it's about my favorite, but nothing happens in it to advance the story."

Right on the target!

Out came the owl scene and the story picked up.

For good measure he had a true ear, a good tenor voice, and when I said, "Bill, let's hear you sing this phrase," would burst into song and "warble" my melody charmingly.

Bill's mathematics, moreover, were flawless; his mental arithmetic almost instantaneous.

I had a background described in the script as the "rolling plains." Bill could not conceive how plains which were by definition flat, could be rolling, which by definition was curved.

Time and again we talked, and got nowhere. He sat at the big table, sulky and helpless, tapping his pencil.

At last I found in the corner of a travel folder a tiny sketch of what I called "rolling plains"—just a few undulating lines that somehow or other gave the effect. I showed it to Bill.

"But that's not *plains*," he objected, "that's *hills*."

"Whatever you call it, that's the way it should look."

By now I was almost hopeless. How could it ever come about that the soul-stretching scene I had in my mind, that infinitely far-reaching expanse of grass, many-shaded, mysterious, beckoning, undulating, could be even faintly suggested on a theatrical backdrop?

It was so easy for Bill, so instantaneous in its execution that, having done it, he promptly forgot it as if nothing of any importance had taken place and gave his whole attention again to the shapes of lightning flashes.

I took pains, later, to discover how the thing was made. It was simply an elevation a few feet high with an irregularly rolling top edge. It was green, of different shades. On it were painted, horizontally, a few long, dark, undulating lines. Placed on stage at the very base of the cyclorama, taking up no space, it delivered the illusion of a hundred miles of rolling grasslands.

This background it was which the audience was to see, really hardly noticing it, when the two sheepherders rose in the morning, performed their ablutions, indulged in some comedy horseplay, and then noticed Windy approaching them from the distance.

Markane Company sent Bill and Vincent Walter out to Cheyenne, Bill to see the sky and cloud effects, the different look of the flat land, the low horizon; Vincent to see to arrangements with the theatre and to discover whether there would be any difficulty about bringing non-unionized musicians to play in a unionized town.

One scene in my script called for a sunrise sky; "the misty blue sky of dawn."

When I first saw this scene ready for rehearsal, it showed the big barn in the background with a flaming red-orange sunset sky behind and above it. This was a couple of weeks before opening date. The scene, Bill assured me, had been painted by the three best scene painters in New York. I did not doubt that. Everything Bill had done was done by the best and the costliest.

I asked if there were any way to soften and dull the redness, and was assured it could be toned down by diminishing the light behind it.

Matt's eyes were on me, in desperation.

"Then let's do that," I said, "tone it down." And Matt added, "Yes! Yes!"

Bill explained it. "That very first night I got out there, in my hotel room, I sat down by the window and looked at the sky. There it was! What I had been hearing about all my life! Those glorious sunsets of the west!"

"Sunsets." I repeated.

"Yes."

"But this was a dawn sky."

Bill hadn't thought that would make any difference —it was sky, it was color, such gorgeous color. He was partial to reds and oranges.

And by the time I saw it there was no time to do anything about it.

This was the trouble all along the line. I was absorbed to the point of exhaustion by work with Dr. Jones. Bill's living and working quarters were in New York. He made weekly or fortnightly trips to Washington to visit the workshop or confer at the university. There was insufficient time, insufficient liaison. Things were done and finished before I had a chance to consider them.

Twenty-Four

THE THEATRE of the Catholic University was an isolated
building across the way from the Music Department in
an empty corner of the campus adjacent to one of the
large boulevards of the city.

It was high enough for two-story sets but not to fly
the curtains; wide enough (twenty-four feet) to withdraw
sets and drops sideways but not with extra room in the
wings; it seated six hundred or so but had no pit for the
orchestra.

Drama students heard lectures in classrooms but the
theatre itself was their workshop. When the Music Department needed it for a show, the time had to be carefully fitted into Father Hartke's schedule, and this done
long in advance.

When Drama put on a show the theatre was available for rehearsals for three weeks before the opening; for
Music, usually one; in our case, two. When I asked Matt
if it didn't worry him he answered in such consternation
that it alarmed me, that it was "terrifying" to think of.

The date of our opening was Wednesday, June 30th.
The play would run for four evenings.

As soon as we were through casting, Matt began rehearsing in any space that was available, empty classrooms or practice rooms or even corridors and halls. For
both Matt (teaching) and our cast (attending regular university classes) this had to be fitted into their daily sched-
ules.

Dr. Paul began to rehearse the choruses.

Sometimes, as I approached the university grounds,
I would hear sounds floating out of the upper windows.
It was thrilling to hear the chorus singing "It's the green
grass!" or "Catch Colt" or "Two locomotives to the top
of the big hill."

Or, the music I heard would be one of the dances,
the "Frolic" or "Swing Your Partner," and I would know
that Frances Nonziato, our choreographer, was rehearsing
the dancing girls. Fran was a wisp of a girl with a rag-doll
body and a halo of tall, stiff black curls. She was the wife
of Bill O'Donnell. Her abilities went way beyond anything she had to do for this show.

Only now, when rehearsals had begun, did Matt
really master the script. The major cutting operation
which I had worked upon it had reduced the original
twenty-seven scenes to sixteen.

The cuts in the music had ruined the neat look of
the piano-vocal scores; they were all marked up, many
pages clipped together to exclude music that was not to
be played. This was very disturbing to me but not to Dr.
Paul or Dr. Bernier, who said it was always so.

Even more disturbing was it to have Matt raise questions about scenes which should have been discussed and
settled long ago.

"Why," he demanded, "do you arrange your scenes

[205]

so monotonously, always the big punch at the end, usually to music? Why not, now and then, begin a scene with music and end up with acting business and comedy?"

This confirmed me in my opinion that Matt was always and primarily the actor, always thinking that the climax would be, not music, but a good bit of business.

I was aghast at the idea of singing an impassioned song when there had been no scene to arouse the passion —yes, nearly all my songs were impassioned or at least full of emotion, emotion which had been generated from the thoughts and speeches of the scene until at last they burst forth in music. To this day I maintain the belief that this is one of the reasons for the effect the music had on audiences.

I struggled to explain. "That would be like getting into a house before you had walked up onto the porch."

He stared at me without comprehension. The idea of a climax being the result of a build-up seemed not to have occurred to him. A climax was just a fine scene, usually full of noise and action. He would like to have the play all climaxes. Build-up scenes were often very quiet. Whatever they did to the audience in the way of creating suspense was indirect, subtle, invisible: to him, not good stage stuff; to me, the most important of all.

His way would have been the right way to stage a revue, but not a story.

We had a long argument about whether or not there should be any reference in the play to the bull. Every dairy herd, of course, has a bull.

"How," he demanded, "did this bull get into the play?"

"Well, one thing leads to another," I explained patiently. "We had to have a chorus of girls, didn't we?"

"We did."

"So we have the milkmaids. And they have to have cows to milk, don't they?"

"Sure."

"So then we have to have a bull."

"No!"

"Certainly. We have to have a bull for the cows."

"But merely implied."

"Well he's only implied in the play."

"No he isn't. You've got him in the dialogue."

"I have not."

"He roars."

"That's not dialogue, that's a sound effect."

"The boys talk about him; that's dialogue."

"Only two lines. Mickey says, 'What's the matter with the cows, making all that rumpus?' And Tim answers, 'The bull's got in with the cows.' "

"Why does he have to get in with them?"

"Oh, Matt, it's an accident! Just a little touch to make the dairy and background convincing. It's the sort of thing that's always happening on a dairy ranch."

Matt, stubbornly, "You do not have to bring that bull on stage."

"But I *don't* bring him on stage!"

"He attacks the boys."

"*Off* stage, not *on!*"

"But the *boys* are on stage! I'll say! When they come flying out of the barn and over the corral fence as if they'd been shot out of a gun!"

"Well, that's how you get stage effects, isn't it?" I was triumphant over this excellent piece of stagecraft. "You have to admit the bull's exciting. And just by hearing the boys speak those lines as they go in the barn, then hearing the thudding hooves, then seeing the boys come shooting out and vaulting over the corral fence, and then that big roar—well, there you are! With a couple of sound effects on a record and two boys making a nice vault, you have an exciting scene."

Matt called the boys. "We'll try it and see what it looks like."

They began, spoke their lines. I objected.

"They sound frightened, the way they said, 'The bull's loose in the barn.'"

"Aren't they frightened?"

"Certainly not."

"But it's a crisis."

"There's no crisis. We don't want a crisis here. We're not building a climax."

"But isn't he dangerous?"

"Of course he is! Everybody knows that!"

"Then why isn't it a crisis?"

"On a ranch that's simply nothing. A daily event. Matt, this is really a comedy scene. You know it's funny. See, you're laughing yourself."

"I'm not laughing at the bull, I'm laughing at you."

"The audience will laugh at the bull even if he does leave you cold."

"He doesn't leave me cold, he frightens me!"

"Oh, Matt He's nothing to be afraid of!"

"*Why* isn't he?"

Exasperated: "But that's just one of the possibilities that are always there, the working conditions of a ranch."

"What a life!"

I finally had to take the bull out, not altogether on account of Matt. I had given Jepson Heath, the owner of the ranch, a line to say when he was alone on stage just after the excitement about the bull. He was to say,

"He is a disturbing element but we can't do without him."

But Jepson Heath delivered this simple remark with a meaning leer.

I corrected the actor quickly, "Oh, no! Not like that! He isn't funny. He doesn't know it's funny."

But this was beyond my actor. Way beyond. If it wasn't funny what was it? The leer would always have been there—in the eye, smile, or voice.

I took the bull out. By this time he terrified me too.

Matt's method of direction was, I have since been told, old-fashioned. He allowed no improvisation whatsoever. He showed the actors how to do it, they were to copy him exactly, learn it by heart, and never deviate.

When he took them, singly, into vacant corners of the university and so taught them, I was seldom present. But when actors and orchestra rehearsed together, in the large instrument room or one of the auditoriums, I attended and in the pauses Dr. Paul and I held whispered conferences about tempi or dynamics—and, of course, those inevitable orchestral mistakes that must be got out of the score *now*.

I saw that Matt came to depend on me a little. He declared himself no musician but he loved it, said to me with shining eyes that when an actor opened his mouth to sing it seemed to him the most exciting moment on stage. We agreed on pace and timing. We both liked it to be fast. We both liked a gay and noisy stage.

If Dr. Paul, conducting, had a different idea, Matt would cast a pleading glance at me. I usually agreed with Matt and would intervene with Dr. Paul. The composer can do this—is, in fact, meant to. But the director cannot. Protocol.

Matt objected to the Spanish Bolero, "I Have a True Love," as too operatic; and I remembered Hoffman's contempt when he exclaimed "Positively operatic!" (Apparently they are all being taught to eschew the operatic.) Matt manoeuvered to leave it out. I countered and put it back.

Matt was wily. I think he intended, in the end, to have his way and was just biding his time. But so was I.

During those winter months there were also many staff conferences about the scenic effects.

The three rainbows, most complicated of all and most important, were to be made in New York. The order was finally given. The price made me gasp.

The lightning flashes and the rainstorm would be electrical effects and could be done by the C. U. technical crew.

My principle concern was still the orchestration.

Since Dr. Jones as well as Hoffman had recommended Charley Cliff, I engaged him to help me finish them.

I had had some fears that Mr. Cliff might want to mutilate my music as Hoffman had done, but I need not have worried. He proved, from the first, an ally. I turned over to him some of the longest and most complicated numbers: the new Overture (new because of the new "medium" orchestra), the "Square Dance" (very fast and noisy), the Scenic Music "Storm," "Rainbows," "Windmill." He obeyed the generally accepted rule: do not change the composer's music; but in arranging it for orchestra he poured on the notes, rivers of black dots covering the pages. He tended to use the greatest possible number of instruments, whereas I used the smallest, preferring a light accompaniment. I liked my way better for the songs, his for the orchestral numbers and dances. Neither of us liked the underscoring which is so much used on Broadway and often makes it difficult, if not impossible, for the audience to hear what is being said on stage.

I learned much from Charley Cliff. We sat beside each other at the opening and had a good time putting our heads together and commenting on the different numbers. "Who did that?" he asked me sharply once. The song was "A Man Can Dream." "I did," I answered. "A good orchestration," he said.

Twenty-Five

HINDSIGHT IS ALWAYS EASY. I should have insisted on more script conferences with Matt, no matter how busy he was or how prejudiced against author's interference.

There were two very serious consequences of my dereliction. The characterization of Joey Bud was wrong. So was that of Letty, the heroine.

In the case of Letty, the mistakes were written in from the beginning. My error. I had not yet learned how frighteningly every slight indication on stage is exaggerated as it comes over the footlights.

I wanted her to be high-spirited, and a little spoiled and wilful, the only child of her parents, their darling, and the darling of the countryside. But on stage, if she stamped her foot and exclaimed *I won't!* she came over as hard and unpleasant; and the better Marilyn acted it, the meaner she seemed.

I wanted her, too, to fall in love with Joey at first sight, and so wrote it. She pled his cause with her mother and father; she went looking for him; she waited around so that she would, accidentally, encounter him. Why should these simple actions have made Hoffman exclaim,

"That girl! Why, she's such a man-chaser." and Dr. Bernier, "A bad girl? Like Carmen?"

And where I had Letty tentatively approach the bunkhouse, waylaying the old cook, Jim, and asking him who was in there having breakfast, Matt, to make bad worse, had her run directly to the door and start to open it. Bold and bad, certainly! A young girl entering the room where the hired hands ate and lived!

Jim seized her from behind and prevented her, exclaiming "Now Letty! You know you can't go into the bunkhouse! Why, the boys is all in there!"

When I first saw this on stage during a rehearsal, it shocked me. I had never written such a thing. But it was done. And I hesitated to try to make Matt re-stage the whole scene and un-teach every actor what he had just taught them.

I believe damage of this sort done to a character early on in the show cannot be undone. I saw echoes of it in the final reviews after Cheyenne.

The characterization of Joey, too, disappointed me. He came over not as a man but as a boy, even childish. Is this the difference between East and West? There has come to be that type called "the strong silent man of the West." Aged twenty, he would be away from home, completely on his own, doing a man's work, dealing with serious things.

Joey was twenty, doing a man's work, but he had frequent angry outbursts; he rattled his lines; he was touchy and temperamental, even to Letty.

Jimmie Gilleran himself was quiet, reserved, well bred, with occasionally a little dry humor. He would only have had to be himself to portray Joey Bud perfectly. But

[213]

this other characterization, undignified, unmanly was, I suppose, imposed upon him to make him more noisy and lively.

Even with this defect he was liked, he was attractive, he was praised. One bit of business I had written for him, that in moments of triumph or excitement he would leap in the air, spread-eagled, with a wild war whoop, he did most effectively.

Another disappointment was the way they talked.

Matt had told me that singers can be taught to act in a few weeks or months but that actors cannot, in the same time, be taught to sing. So we would be having a cast of singers and his big job would be to make actors of them.

He really did wonders in making them act but their speaking remained terrible. Let them open their mouths and sing, and it was gorgeous; but to speak! Diction, enunciation, inflexions deplorable.

(I have heard that at the Metropolitan Opera they have the same trouble).

Several of our cast had picked up the common modern trick of very fast speech, so fast they can hardly be understood. They rattled. I begged Matt to make them speak decently.

Matt exclaimed, "I wish you'd tell me what to say to them to make them do that!"

I began to hear anxious remarks from Dr. Paul, from Matt and Vincent about the slow opening when Joey first sings a song off-stage then enters and has a talk with Jim, the bunkhouse cook.

This was my responsibility of course, I had written it that way and it *was* slow—the always troublesome exposition. But in my opinion it was absolutely necessary to make what followed understandable. Audience *had* to know that the sheepherders were wealthy fugitives from justice, else when they entered and did their funny stuff it would not be funny. Audience *had* to know the dairy-owner's belief that unless all his little milkmaids were good girls the cows would not let down their milk, else, similarly, the lively scene when the milkmaids entered would misfire.

I felt the audience would accept it, as one is always willing to accept a few slow pages at the beginning of a book while one is becoming acquainted with the characters. Vincent agreed with me.

Matt wanted the whole scene dropped. Begin with the entrance of the milkmaids and their slapstick and dancing. But I was sure the scene would fall flat unless it was prepared. Matt insisted. I refused. Vincent and I stuck to our guns, but we worried about it.

The University was putting out publicity and arranging interviews. A social evening at the Washington Press Club was arranged, during the course of which Jimmie went up on stage and sang two songs out of the show: "Green Grass of Wyoming" and "Little White Nightie." They both came over well at this informal party, and presently a journalist had taken the seat beside me and we were talking. He had once been a drama critic. He told me he would attend our First Night. He told me too that he could tell when a show would be a winner. He predicted this one would be.

"That song," he motioned to Jimmie up on the stage, "That song will do it. You'll see, now. It will go to Broadway."

Father Hartke did us a good turn that winter. Since no one was producing operettas, nor Americana, he said it would be practically a necessity to break the news to the public somehow in the title, or subtitle.

So I devised the subtitle, "A Folk Tale of the Western Plains with Music." This begged a good many sensitive questions and has served us well.

By the time we got into the theatre to rehearse, everything was pretty well set except the rainbows, the lightning flashes, the rain.

Bill was not in the least concerned; they would be ready in time for the show, why begin to worry now?

"How do you know they will?"

"They've promised."

I was to find this artless faith in promises over and over again in my technical director. He was surprised that anyone should worry until the actual moment came. Dr. Paul and I looked at each other in despair.

Does one really believe that way when one is twenty-two?

Bill didn't even think it was important to try to get a glimpse of things in advance. It would be all right and it would come in time, so why worry?

"But I can show you the rain any time—would you like to see it now?"

I certainly would.

I sat in the dark theatre and saw the rain—a shimmering sheet of slanting, moving dot-and-dash lines of light and shadow, through which one could glimpse whatever was behind.

I knew I must often before have seen rain on stage at plays or operas. I wondered if it had been this same species. It was a suggestion, yes, a bare suggestion, of wetness and water but I doubted if, when I had first thought

[216]

of pouring rain, I would have gone on with it if I had known that this was the best that could be done.

But did it matter too much? The wind effects—the windmill spinning so fast, the lightning flashes, and, after all, only a few seconds of rain, the whole storm scene from the first downpour when everyone runs screaming from the stage, through all the rain and crashing and blazing of lightning clear to the last quiet rainbow only took a couple of minutes—the rain would do, I thought, it would get by. Accepted as one of those stage conventions which fall far short of convincingness but are constantly used.

I did not like it.

I saw, now, the danger of every difficult scenic effect.

The novice receives the opposite advice. Put "gimmicks" in. An unusual one might give a director his first advancement. And don't worry about how it can be done. Almost anything can be done.

No, was my conclusion. Perhaps one or two, and not too difficult. In this play, to be done by a university, one would have been enough: the windmill. And for the rest, the simpler the better.

A good many of our rehearsals were still done without all the props or sets. These were being got ready.

In the Broadway theatre, styles in scene-shifting keep changing. At present the elaborate machinery which rotates the scenes on a hidden underground turntable is the latest thing.

I myself don't like it. It makes too much of a mere means to an end. I prefer the minimum of machinery to create the illusion. I like the Chinese method: the actor, walking across the floor, suddenly gives a small hop, and continues. This conveys to the audience that he has stopped over a threshold and entered a different room. More imagination. Less mechanics.

A few years ago they shifted scenery by having stage-hands enter in full sight of the audience and move the sets around.

Audiences liked it; though, for the moment, the illusion was broken and the audience together with the story-teller stood outside the story.

Possibly that is the reason this method has gone out of style.

Today, sets and props remove themselves from stage without visible help.

Suppose the right hand wall of the stage is the front of a house. It slides backward and out of sight. Furniture also; and if the pieces are large it is clever and practical. But to see small pieces suddenly come to life, move across stage under their own power and exit is simply a scream. And audience screamed. The long bench, midstage, suddenly decides to leave the stage—and does so. To make it funnier, Joey is lying on it flat on his back.

But when I complained to Bill he stood his ground. It is the right way to move props nowadays.

And anyway, it was all done, and couldn't be changed.

I wondered if anything at all could safely be changed at this late date.

Once or twice, when I tackled Matt he gave me a little lecture about creating uncertainty in the actors just when, at last, he had brought them to the point of certainty in their parts.

I had some experience of this with Jimmie Gilleran's

songs. He could not sing an F-sharp. There were several in his part and I was obliged to change his melodic line. When he had learned it the new way, I changed it again. And then again. Jimmie was a nervous wreck.

It was some comfort to remember that this Washington performance was, after all, just a try-out. The first try-out. The second would be at Cheyenne and there would be an interval of seven weeks between the two. Blessed *time* in which Matt and I could really get together and iron out the discrepancies.

I started writing a new script with copious notes. The play, next time, would have a better shape. Devise smoother, easier scene changes. Correct the characterizations of Joey and Letty. Do over the ridiculous milking scene. And the slow opening? Sometimes a slow opening can be made tolerable by putting a short, lively scene before it. I began to think about this.

Criticisms are valuable, even one's own. But there is always that tendency to see the bad and never the good. Whereas, actually, it is what is good in a play that might bring it ultimate success, irrespective of what is bad. Bad things little by little can be eliminated.

So I looked for the good and it brought a smile to my face: the gaiety, the pace, the fresh, laughing young faces, and the lilting music that carried all along; the high, soaring notes, and a definite interest in the story which somehow came over even through the disconnected scenes of the rehearsals.

I remembered; music 40%, story 40%, visual effects 20%.

Everyone was talking about the music.

And the actors—the singers—one by one they came

to me and spoke of the melodies, of the duet of Letty and Joey when they sing the "evocation of the wind."

See all the aspen, quaking in their boots!
Shiverin' and shakin' right down to their roots!
See all the clouds a-sailin' in the sky!
Where's the wind they're sailing by?

The wild, whooping yells they give when the windmill begins to move!

And the other melodies! John Miller poured forth his wonderful tones as Windy, singing,

"Just about so high I think he'd be."

And that was when Dr. Bernier slipped into the seat beside me in the dark theatre and said, quietly, "Beautiful music, Mary."

Twenty-Six

OPENING DAY, Wednesday, May 31st., moved close.

There was something I had never known: that you cannot get an audience into a theatre without a name star to draw them in.

There was a term I had never heard: "paper the house."

There was something I had not realized: that the day before our opening was a holiday, Memorial Day. Not a shop would be open or a workman on hand for last-minute necessities. Moreover, many businesses were giving their employees the Monday off, too, so there would be a four-day vacuum.

On the previous Thursday I had not yet seen a rainbow or a lightning flash nor was our record of sound effects ready.

Friday was dress rehearsal and I saw a lightning flash—a section of sky about a yard square which began to blink on and off feebly. You hardly noticed it.

The storm music was not bad but needed much more rehearsing. The rainbows were still absent.

Dr. Jones sat beside me and I heard his kind and quiet voice, "The storm is your weakest point."

Matt came to me, tense and urgent. "We'd better cut out the storm." It was in everybody's mind.

Bill's face was white. "Over my dead body!" He was looking at me. A question dawned in his eyes. "And your's too, Miss O'Hara?"

Such a storm as crashed and thundered in my mind every time I thought of it, such as I had put into the script, such as I had often written for the screen *could* be put on a theatrical stage. I still believe it. But there would be needed plenty of time, much money and experimentation, a skilled and experienced crew who had nothing else to think of.

But it could not be done now, not in any way to be proud of or even half satisfied with. Perhaps for Cheyenne?

The storm would have to come out.

"The rainbows!" protested Dr. Paul. They had been paid for.

But obviously, no storm, no rainbows. I got to work cutting the script again.

It was fortunate that the first act had a sort of double peak to the climax.

> The first was: getting the windmill up, getting it spinning, getting everyone on stage singing and dancing in triumph. (All this went well.)

> The second was: the wind which has risen in response to Joey's and Letty's singing, keeps getting stronger, brings the storm, drives everyone from the stage, then subsides; then come the rainbows, and everyone runs back on stage.

The scene finished with a chorus which could be tacked on to the end of the first peak as easily as the second. Then curtain and intermission.

Dr. Paul, Dr. Jones, and I went over the score, making the big cuts; also through the extracted parts for the orchestra.

The continuity of the key scheme was broken; I had to alter some measures here. It was a little abrupt but not a noticeable break.

Bill worked at the sound effects handicapped by the fact that parts were still missing and not a radio shop in town was open. He finally got what he needed and the result, both for Washington and Cheyenne, was superb.

Friends of mine were coming into town for the opening: Peggy, Marian, Ethel, Barbara, Edna, Helen, Elma, Comfort, the Eldridges, the Coverts. My Georgetown house filled up.

I have since heard that all producers see to it that the theatre, on opening night, is well filled. Unless there is such a drawing card as a big name star, arrangements are made in advance. Sometimes the whole cast of another show is invited in. Or groups of students. C. U. often filled seats with members of other Catholic organizations.

We should have, but did not. If my name was supposed to be a sufficient drawing card, it proved a disappointment. We had only a fair house on opening night, a worse house the next night (I went to sleep), slightly better the third, and quite decidedly better on the fourth and last, Saturday.

The performance did really pick up during those four nights.

There were newspaper critics present on the first night. Dr. Paul had invited them and sent them tickets. This is always done, I hear. I can't see why.

Who is there, who has seen an original play brought

[223]

to the point of production—so many ideas proved impractical or ineffective, loose ends tied up as best they might be—who would expect to see flawless theatre on opening night? And, since there must be flaws, why expect critics not to notice and land on them?

I had heard as much talk as anyone else about bad criticisms closing shows but I had never taken them too seriously.

Also, when Harold Freedman had said he would send New York managers down to Washington to see our show, there had been, in his mind, a condition. Provided, he meant, it got a good review on the first night.

And this good review, I learned later, must be from Richard Coe, dramatic critic on the *Washington Post*. No other Washington critic counted for so much. Mr. Coe was invited, sent a ticket; he came.

There was also present, drawn by the title, *Oh! Wyoming!*, a critic who had formerly been on the *State Tribune* of Cheyenne, Wyoming. He wrote a review of the piece, mostly just factual data about the story and the staff, and at the end a single flat statement, adulatory enough to take your breath away:

After the show, praise of the music was unanimous.

Why such a statement was not noticed or commented upon more than it was, has puzzled me. Consider the Broadway openings. After what proportion of those does one ever read the critical statement that praise of the music was unanimous? But there it was—written, printed, published and copied widely. What success has followed *Oh! Wyoming!* I attribute largely to this statement.

Up until the last moment I had been immersed in

work on orchestrations. Working on music removes one from actual living. I was in a daze, still in a daze when I went to the theatre that night, and all through the play.

If I had been asked afterwards, "Well, how did it go?" I would have answered, "Just wonderfully!"

I was immensely relieved that there were no breakdowns. Jimmie remembered his new melodic lines; the roughness that scarred the ending of the first act climax was noticed by no one but me, I felt sure; there were far more laughs than I had expected; interest in the story held to the end; and there was no doubt about enthusiasm for the music.

In the intermission and afterwards I was surrounded by groups of congratulating people, many of them friends of mine, many newly introduced. Beaming faces! Predictions of all kinds of glory! Hands and shoulder squeezed.

Matt, meeting me afterwards, said with a trace of sourness "This first-night audience must be a confirmed lot of opera lovers." "Why?" I asked. "Because of the way they applauded 'I Have a True Love.' It almost stopped the show."

I, too, had noticed that. They simply would not stop clapping.

I went to bed that night in a rosy haze. I woke in the morning in a wonderful let-down feeling of having really got over the high hurdle and went to the mail box. In it was a letter which had been delivered by hand.

It was pleasant to open it and see a strange handwriting. For a moment I didn't recognize the signature. Then I saw it was the name of the newspaper man who had sat beside me at the Press Club party.

The note was a congratulation. He had been unable

[225]

to go to the opening of *Oh! Wyoming!* himself (he suffered from arthritis) but he had sent his eighteen-year-old daughter, with instructions to come to his room when she returned and tell him all about it.

He wrote, ". . . I thought you would like to hear this. She sat down on the edge of my bed and said, *'Daddy, it was darling'.*"

He signed his name and added, "my prediction still stands."

And having read that I thought that my modest hopes for the show—that it would provide the theatregoer with a pleasant evening's entertainment—had really materialized.

It was about then that I got the first telephone call telling me that I was being slaughtered by the reviews.

In due time I procured them and sat down to read them. No single good thing was said and I wondered why. If a stranger from out of town had seen and heard "after the show praise of the music was unanimous" a Washington critic with eyes and ears open must have seen and heard the same thing.

If he didn't comment on it, it must have been because he did not want to give any praise at all. This being the case, it was never in the cards for us to get it from him.

Every one of the reviews was written in the spirit of smart city boys sniggering at country rubes. They gibed and ridiculed. Was this why Father Hartke had warned us to announce in advance that the play was about "folk"?

Richard Coe even made a little playlet of his review, casting himself in the role of one of the rubes, saying "Gee—Bud's a reel popular name—" and "milkmaids! gad, I fergot to mention THEM" and "I figgered . . ."

and "by gosh . . ." He threw some nasty barbs at the C. U. Music Department but the heavy guns were all for me on the score that I had stolen "dollops" from *Oklahoma,* stolen the multiple sets from *Donnybrook,* the windmill going up from *Wildcat* and *Plain and Fancy,* Joey's "superman" achievements from *Li'l Abner,* the fatherless boy from *Gilbert and Sullivan,* the suddenly snobbish heroine from *Oscar Wilde.*

The music, too, had a long list of ancestors: Lehar, Kallman, Weil, and Ferde Grofé.

On first reading the impact was stinging.

Ridicule! That extraordinary weapon. And extraordinary, too, that small boys have become the master of it. Every child that has been through school knows that if two or three others, with sneering grins and pointing fingers, announce that he has come to school with his sister's sweater on, he becomes a pariah.

But on second reading the reviews lost a good deal of their virulence; it was so apparent that they were not serious. The writers were giving themselves a very good time at our expense, wisecracking.

Marilyn was the only one who received praise. "Only Marilyn Landers, a skilled veteran . . . struck me as at home in her chores. She performed and sang with wide-eyed zeal."

Dr. Paul and Mike Cordovana were already congratulating themselves and me and the whole music department on that thrilling tribute from Cheyenne:

After the show, praise of the music was unanimous

The last night, Saturday, was the best night. Why attendance should have picked up after those reviews I cannot imagine, but it did; there was a happy and confident spirit in the cast; Dr. Paul got the best performance out of the orchestra that they had yet given and as I walked up to congratulate him, I saw by his countenance, streaming with perspiration, and impassive as ever (I was learning how to read that poker-face), that he felt we had come through with a creditable offering.

Twenty-Seven

ALL OF THE CRITICISMS, both of the newspapers and our own "gang", must now be most carefully considered, for the show in Cheyenne, at its second try-out, would have its new shape and it must be flawless.

First of all, I wanted to correct the characterizations of Joey and Letty. But Matt advised most strongly against this. The kids, he said, (Marilyn and Jimmie) were letter-perfect in the old way. Altering characterizations meant altering the way every scene was acted, every line spoken. There wouldn't be time. It was not only dangerous, it was impossible. Between now and Cheyenne, school would close, the whole cast would scatter.

I gave it up. I was sorry. It meant a good deal, I thought, to the play. It must wait, then, for the third tryout.

"What about the storm?" Matt asked. "I hope you're not considering putting that back in?"

When I said I was (because we had the rainbows, we had the music, we had seven weeks) he shook his head.

Matt had just taken on some important extracurricular activity. He had staged a floor show for one of the more extravagant restaurants, the "Rive Gauche", and was playing an act in it himself, he and his beautiful wife. This meant theatrical hours for them, working at night, sleeping till noon.

"I wouldn't have time now," he said. "It would have to be done in Cheyenne."

In Cheyenne we would know nothing about technicians, supplies, workshops. Bill would have to go out long in advance.

I looked into Matt's eyes. They were very steady, very determined. "I strongly advise against it," he said.

It did not take me a minute to realize he was right. Besides, the closing scene of Act One had gone very well. Apparently we did not need the double-peaked climax.

The milking scene would of course have to be corrected. I trembled to think what Cheyenites—country people, really, many of them living on farms outside town—would think about those cows with tails up in the air.

But this was just a paint job. It could be done in Cheyenne. I could plan it now, rewrite the script in detail, have it ready for Bill when he went out.

I wanted to do away with the excess of sets and props but again I was stopped by practical considerations. All this was the articulated machinery that kept the show rolling, kept one scene following the next from beginning to end. To tear it all out and substitute another scheme with different parts and cogs! No, it couldn't be done.

Again, I said to myself: well, then, for the third tryout.

One reviewer, I think it was the *Daily News,* had been very sarcastic about the number of times the plot was stated: ". . plot announced, of course, the full three times—just as the school books direct."

But this reviewer missed a few. Yes, actually, I had so greatly feared that my audience would fail to catch the all-important beginnings of the plot that with my usual over-carefulness, I had hammered it home.

Vincent looked at me gravely. "Yes, Miss O'Hara— seven times."

"Not seven times, Vincent?"

"Yes, seven times."

Driving home on the New Jersey Turnpike, through New York, out on the Merritt Parkway, I thought it all over. There was not, after all, so very much that could be done between now and Cheyenne. The play was neither on stage nor in rehearsal. The cast would reassemble in Cheyenne a certain number of days before the opening with Matt to direct them. Bill, Vincent, and probably Dr. Paul would go out before that. The fewer changes I initiated now the better.

Many miles went under the wheels while I thought about that.

There was, for instance, the matter of all the dialogue.

I knew now—Oh, how well I knew it—what I had wondered about so long ago, perhaps when I was driving on this very parkway.

Should I give them plenty of words? Or the minimum?

Should it be just "mighty dry season" or the forty words in which the cook had complained to Joey that because of lack of water the ditches were drying up, etc., and etc., and etc.

What was true of my cast here at C. U. would be true of any cast that ever played this show. They would be singers, not drama students or actors. No actors could sing it.

Therefore, don't kid yourself by thinking that you will ever have a group that can speak well, enunciate, place their voices properly for speech, or even make themselves understood. They'll gabble, swallow the tail of every sentence, rattle, run it all together.

Ergo: cut the dialogue to the bone.

This, I thought, I could certainly do now, between the two shows and began, with great pleasure, to do it. Amazing, how the same story that, it had seemed, could only be told in a thousand words, discovers itself neatly and clearly told in a hundred.

But here again I was foiled. For when would they have time to re-learn the entire play?

This too would have to be postponed for the third try-out.

There was one change, however, which could and should be made.

The Senator from Wyoming had been present at our first night. His verdict, "Very good. Very promising, except for the slow opening."

He would be in Cheyenne before we were. Out there they would ask him about the show. He would carry the word. They would know before we got there that there was an ineffectual opening.

A Catholic Monsignor had been present. He had liked it, he said, could criticize only the slow opening. "Begin with the milkmaids," he said.

Dr. Paul had repeated it to me, looking at me inquiringly. "Begin with the milkmaids?"

But it was impossible to begin with the milkmaids, for before they appeared you had to know about them, about the sheepherders, about Letty. And these three subjects were dealt with in that "slow" talk between the cook and Joey.

What you *could* do, was introduce another scene before it.

As the story went, the boy rides into the ranch at sunrise, singing. Girl wakes and hears him. Why not show that? She flings back covers, goes to window, looks out. Why not show that? Then begins quickly to dress, so that she can go down and see who this stranger is. Why not show that?

I visualized the opening. The theatre going dark, after the overture. Presently, off-stage, Joey's voice singing. Then, about halfway up the big curtain, a spot of light and small curtains in the big curtain open, showing a young girl's bedroom; Letty, in bed, wakes, sits up, listens, runs to the window and looks out; song stops (for Joey is there below); she runs back to bed, sits on the edge and begins to draw on her stockings.

Now blackout, music proceeds, big curtain up. There is the white-aproned cook ringing the breakfast bell. Joey walks into the scene.

I was sure, now, the audience would be ready to listen to him talking, asking questions, the cook giving the answers, especially about the girl he had seen at the window. And it couldn't drag, because we've seen her ourselves, our leading lady, we've seen her in an intimate setting, her bedroom; we've seen her waking from sleep, in her little white nightie; we know she's heard Joey's song,

[233]

seen him below her window; we know she's interested.

Though I had been thinking about this scene since the dress rehearsal, I had not yet said anything to Matt about it. I wanted to be sure. I worked out every detail, every prop, every angle. Every time I managed to forget it, then came to it again fresh (the best way for testing), it gave me the lift I wanted; it rang a little bell: this is it.

One day, in my writing room at Tyrawley, I carefully wrote out the new pages, then got Matt long distance on the telephone.

"It's about the opening, Matt—that long expository scene."

"Yes, I know. Begin with the milkmaids."

"No, I've got another. . . ."

"But why bother with anything else? It's a good scene. Everybody likes the milkmaids."

"But the trouble is, Matt. . . ."

"At the university, they were all saying that—you ought to begin with the milkmaids. I've always said so."

"Now listen, Matt. . . ."

"I can't talk very long. Couldn't this be left until we get out to Cheyenne?"

"No, not possibly."

"Why not?"

"Because I'll need another set and Bill will have to. . . ."

"My God! Not another set!"

"Matt, I wish you'd listen!"

"I wish *you* would! Begin with the milkmaids! That'll solve all the problems, and you can give some of those lines. . . ."

"Matt you're acting as if you didn't want to hear anything about it."

Matt, after a moment's pause, said, "I've got an awful lot on my mind."

"Well then, shall I just send it to you?"

"You've got it all written?"

"Yes, it's finished."

"All right, send it to me."

"And when you've read it, call me back?"

"Call you back?"

"Yes, if you've got anything you want to say or argue about."

So it was left and, with relief that the die was cast, I called up Bill O'Donnell and we began to talk about how that small upper bedroom could be built behind the big curtain, and what the furniture should be—in that era girls liked to have bird's-eye maple furniture, or perhaps a brass bed. And that little white nightie; since, now, the nightie was to be seen, we must think about it. Bill wanted to design one. I gave him permission, though doubting that it would look much like what a country girl would wear on a Wyoming ranch. In any case, it must conform to the lyric Joey sings about it,

> That little white nightie—so prissy
> With tucking in front—very neat;
> Sleeves down to here
> Blue ribbons here
> Then long and straight to her feet

Bill, in due time, sent me the sketch of the nightie —such a nightie as never was on land or sea. With it came the estimate of a top-notch (he assured me of that) costumer, promising to make the garment for $100.

I did not take up with this offer but went hunting instead for nighties all over New York. But no such simple and dainty little nightie was to be found, so at last I bought the fine white nainsook and cut and hand-sewed the nightie myself, as, when I was nineteen and engaged to be married, I had hand-made the nighties for my own trousseau.

The thrill I felt about this new opening scene was the sort of thrill one feels when inspecting some brand-new, inspired creation and finding it good.

I do not customarily look for the silver lining in clouds. In fact, people who do rather annoy me. I feel that in the face of disappointment it is more honest and more human to grouch, even to swear.

All the same, if the reviews of *Oh! Wyoming!* had been favorable, and a New York manager *had* come to Washington to see it, and *had* liked and bought it, I would not now have had the chance of making the second shape, which I knew in advance was going to be so much better than its first shape. I would probably have had little or nothing to do with it.

Having begun it, I want to finish it myself and feel that it is right.

Twenty-Eight

WHILE, AT TYRAWLEY, I worked at the new scene and the nightie, keeping in close touch with Bill. Dr. Paul and his assistants were dealing with logistics. It was like planning for an army. Any idea of chartering buses or planes had been abandoned. Traveling expenses would be allotted and everyone would go west in whatever manner they pleased.

Understudies for all the principle parts must be provided. Dr. Paul and I discussed this by telephone. Barbara Ann Thompson as understudy for the part of Letty: a girl with an elfin, elusive personality and a small, exquisite, high, very true voice. Not so much volume as Marilyn, not so much experience, but a musician. She would easily be able to master the part.

And John Philibert as understudy for Jimmie Gilleran. I groaned at this thought for John was a low baritone, nearly a bass, and Jimmie's voice was considerably higher. More trouble for me with range and melodic lines. But John was handsome and magnetic and outstanding. There was no other.

Dr. and Mrs. Ryan, parents of our star dancing girl

would drive her out in the family car and remain for the duration, an arrangement that was delightful for everyone. They became Mommy and Daddy of the show.

Dr. Paul told me of the acquisition of a new cellist, very much needed, a young fellow who played in the National Symphony Orchestra. He wanted to go west for a visit with his family. He played the counter melody in "Little White Nightie"—and how beautifully!

He told me, later, that he and others of the National Symphony Orchestra had discussed the musical numbers of my show. They liked the music, particularly "Little White Nightie" and "Top o' the Big Hill."

We were going to need more musicians than we had. Dr. Paul arranged with Cheyenne by telephone to provide us with a number, engaging them (anxiously) sight unseen or, rather, sound unheard. He need not have worried. Every one surpassed his expectations. A number of strings, a trombonist, and a tall girl from Denver—the best double bass we had had.

Later, the violinists told him it was a pleasure to play with us, that they did not often get a chance to play such good music.

Accommodations for all—cast, orchestra, staff—were taken at the "Hitching Post," an attractive four-square motel with swimming pool in center just outside of town. Space was ample, restaurant excellent, extra halls for rehearsals available. Dates of arrival for each person were set.

Vincent and Bill would go out first.

Dr. Paul planned to drive out in his big blue station wagon with his wife and the three youngest of his five children. It is lucky he did so. I was to see that car,

[238]

crammed with actors, children, musicians and their instruments, shuttling from Hitching Post to Lincoln Theatre and back many times a day.

Marilyn Landers had another theatrical engagement
just before our opening and would not arrive till the last
minute. This worried all of us, but Marilyn arrived by
plane with a few hours to spare.

Matt posed a difficulty for he was still playing in his
show at the "Rive Gauche". He could spare us just five
days. He would rehearse and drill our cast for those five
days, then leave before opening night.

There was one important change which I kept to
myself till the last moment. This was the change of title.

I had no intention of continuing handicapped by the
possibility, really a probability, that when anyone heard
our title, *Oh! Wyoming!* they would counter with, *Oh!
Klahoma!*

No matter how commercial Jean Dalrymple had
considered *Oh! Wyoming!* my first instinct against it (as
too similar to Oklahoma) had been right. Why invite ad-
verse comment? There were other titles. I feared *Catch
Colt* because, though it looks stunning written (imagine
it in lights over a theatre) yet, spoken, it does sound like
"catch cold."

Top O' the Big Hill, I thought; the name of the song
that was just about the most popular of all, the one near
the end which people thought ought to have a *réprise.* (I
thought so too, but could find no place for it). And it
means, "the Rocky Mountain Divide."

But publicity was already pouring out in Cheyenne
for *Oh! Wyoming!* It was, of course, coupled with the
publicity for "Frontier Days." Sister shows they were,

bracketted together, an afternoon show and an evening one. The town was plastered with posters, the air rang with twin announcements. The Frontier Committee were certainly keeping their word to us. How could I change the title now? How could I even mention the new one?

I decided it could not be done until opening night. Then, at the last minute, *Oh! Wyoming!* would come down, and *Top O' the Big Hill* go up. Newspapers would comment upon it. Inside the theatre we would have a new title curtain.

Bill and I discussed this by telephone while I was at Tyrawley. He sent me the sketch which I approved, and he then painted one of the finest jobs he had done for me: a red-orange sky (again!) above a silhouetted mountain line—irregular crags jutting up and, reaching up from them, the black skeleton outline of a windmill. Above this, upon the red sky, the black letters of the new title, *Top O' the Big Hill.*

Dr. Paul was receiving bids from various moving companies for the job of transporting our scenery and props and finally gave the contract. Arrangements were made, dates set, the vans would pick up the stuff from the workshop and from the university. Props included twenty-two newly purchased metal folding reading stands with lights for the musicians (Dr. Paul's pride). They were left out in a conspicuous place to be fitted into the van. What happened was that they were overlooked, walked around as it were, forgotten, and left behind.

When at last Kent and I took our places in the plane and flew off, facing west, my thoughts outdistanced the plane, wondering if Marilyn would arrive in time for rehearsals; how the new opening, the little bedroom scene would pan out; if Matt was already there, rehearsing, as he was supposed to be. . . .

Twenty-Nine

MATT WAS THERE.

I had hardly settled into my room at the Hitching Post when he came to see me.

"I have a suggestion to make," he said.

"What is it?"

"Let's open the show with the milkmaids."

I stared at him. I just couldn't believe it.

"And what about the bedroom scene?"

He looked puzzled.

"Matt! You remember the new scene I sent you the script of!"

I spelled it out. Reminded him of our talk on the telephone when I was at Tyrawley and he in Washington. "If you didn't like the bedroom scene why didn't you say so before I had spent three thousand dollars having the set built and shipped?"

Matt was stupefied.

Well, no use drawing out the agony. He had not read the script, knew nothing about the bedroom scene, had been busy with other things, and had just laid it aside and forgotten it.

He was chagrined and apologetic which helped me in resisting his next havoc-wreaking suggestion: that we remove the first act climax, the windmill scene, from the end of the first act and put it at the beginning of the second act.

Here he was again, trying to get into the house before he had gone up onto the porch.

His argument was that all the big producers change their scenes around on the eve of opening, so we ought to do likewise.

I wondered if he could be serious. A climax being, to my mind, inseparable from the step-by-step build-up to it, I saw half of the first act dissolving into nothing.

"And how would you fill in all that space?" I asked.

"You could write some stage business."

"When?"

"Right now."

It was like Mrs. Tuttle, in Hollywood, saying, "Why that will be for *you* to do, Miss O'Hara." And I answered Matt with the same words. "You overestimate my powers."

Matt had called me a pushover when, long ago, I had so quickly acceded to his request that I leave out the Swedes.

I was not a pushover this time. I was inwardly shuddering at the terrible vision of my whole play falling to pieces like a house of cards.

I said no.

A tug-of-war between Matt and me was, after all, nothing new. Fortunately, and I don't know quite why, we always emerged better friends with better understanding, more mutual respect.

He even complimented me after rehearsal a few nights later. "I think you've got a hit after all!"

"What do you mean, 'after all'?"

"Well, I've never thought so before."

"What's happened now?"

"Your music. That gang of western people who were at the rehearsal, they mobbed me! Just crazy about it."

They had mobbed me, too.

And when we drove Matt to the airport a few hours before the show was to open, he made a declaration.

"I've always said the only good writer is a dead writer. I now make one exception. Everything you've done to the show has helped it."

He was referring, of course, to the new opening. Letty's little bedroom scene. Yes, everyone agreed it was an improvement. I thought so, too. But I was disappointed in it. (At this stage, I kept this to myself.) It was better, but not enough better. Not just right. Too complicated. That small scene opening off the big curtain like a peephole—after all, just another gimmick to my credit (or loss).

"All aboard!"

"Matt I wish you weren't leaving. I don't see how we'll get along without you. Suppose something goes wrong?"

"Nothing'll go wrong. Why," with a big grin, *"your show's on!"*

He grabbed me. "I'm no kisser, but here goes!"

This was Matt's exit.

On the heels of Matt's first visit to me at the Hitching Post had come Bill's. He was almost despairing. He pled with me not to change the milking scene.

(Oh, my heavens! The farmers! The Cheyenne dairymen! Those uplifted tails!)

But he insisted, item by item, showing me the impossibility of getting it done in time and properly rehearsed.

I gave in. All right, then, tails up! It had to be a comedy scene. (It was.)

One after another they came to me with their troubles.

At first the orchestra had been so affected by the altitude they had no wind and could not rehearse. The oboe reeds collapsed. The woodwinds and brass lay flat on the floor, gasping.

As we got closer to opening night I became aware of conflicts and misunderstandings all around me. Something besides the milking scene was wrong with Bill. He says, now, he hopes he will never have to go through anything like *that* again. (What?)

Dr. Paul, who is not a nervous man, begins to shudder and wring his hands when Bill is mentioned. (What goes on?)

They've given Bill a nickname: The Hollywood Producer.

Matt and Bill were not on speaking terms.

At the end of a talk I had with Bill and Vincent, Bill suddenly exclaimed, "Mary O'Hara, I'll follow you to the ends of the earth!" and from the emotion in his voice I gauged the depth of his distress. But I still don't know what it was about.

One bit of romance brightened the atmosphere. Our leading man and Patricia, in charge of props, fell in love. They are now married.

Kirk Knox, critic and columnist on the *Wyoming*

State Tribune, asked for an interview with me in preparation for writing his review of the play and came to my room at a time when I, with help from Jimmie and John and Pat (all seated on the floor), was copying into the sixteen piano-vocal books some small changes I had just made. The bed was covered with orchestrations and extracted parts.

Seated on a suit case, Kirk Knox kept scribbling notes, now and then interpolating a question.

When they left we talked for an hour.

He told me, regretfully, that he knew nothing about music, nor had any particular feeling for it, so his comments must deal with other aspects of the show.

And so we moved toward the big night, a small world of our own, circling within the larger world of the town.

Thirty

Recognition is ninety percent.

When, in the nineteen-thirties, I first saw the epic grandeur and beauty of the Wyoming plains, I was thrilled; and wrote the three Flicka books.

At that time a young Polish farmer commented, "I've lived here most of my life but I had never seen any of that beauty. Now I read those books, and go out and look around, *and I see it!*"

He sent me a message of thanks.

Thanks and appreciation have been coming to me ever since, a tidal wave of it, and from all over the world. But not only to me. Also to Wyoming and to Cheyenne and now it was bouncing back to me again. Cheyenne opened its arms to me and welcomed me back. I've never been so interviewed, photographed, written about, escorted, be-ribboned and be-flowered in my life.

Besides this public acclaim there was the great pleasure of my reunions with dear friends of long ago.

The town was in fiesta.

When summer comes in the East, people escape from the stifling heat of cities to the mountains and oceanside. In the West it is just the opposite. From the empty plains and the highlands and foothills, the lonely outriders hurry to town. As the week of the big Rodeo approaches Cheyenne fills up. Streets are jammed with autos between which galloping pinto ponies weave their way, riders whooping. Banners float overhead; announcers stand on street corners with megaphones.

This year they proclaimed not only the Frontier Park attraction but also the "World Premiere" of Mary O'Hara's Musical Play.

Posters, pamphlets, fliers, photographs everywhere.

The town bubbled with parties. Engagements for me had been made in advance. The Governor of Wyoming was my partner at many. At our first night he stood on the stage beside me and bestowed red roses on me.

Was it a success this time?

That depends on the point of view from which the question is asked.

"Our hearts were lighter when we had seen it."

This word of approval came in a manner of speaking from Europe, specifically from Vienna, for there was a Viennese Baroness, together with other cosmopolitans, visiting at a Denver house party.

I met them all at a dinner party. They were going to the show, would talk it over afterwards, and send word to me what the consensus of opinion was: a really international opinion.

In due time the Baroness delivered it. She had seen theatrical openings everywhere, she said, so they could believe her when she declared that this was really good. It really had the makings (though it needed more sex), the particularly good thing about it being the wry, dry philosophy of the old man who sang

When you get what you want you don't want it!
When you want what you want you don't get it!
What you really do want is to want—and to WANT!
So go right on wanting—you've got it!

Other good opinions buzzed around my head like a swarm of bees. A crowd of Texans leaped from their car and surrounded me on the street. "Your—show—is —MAGNIFICENT!"

Favorable opinions reached Dr. Paul every night after the show: always the same, "Beautiful music." with compliments for the orchestrations, particularly the use of the French horn.

How quickly the word-of-mouth comments spread, like the Wyoming wind that blows over the plains! Months later I was to receive a letter from Oklahoma ". . . when I was visiting in Wyoming last summer the state was buzzing with the success of your musical . . . hope it has a long run. . . ."

The newspaper comments were favorable. Kirk Knox wrote in the *Wyoming State Tribune,* "A pleasant evening's entertainment." And I thought, Well! Well! Here we are at last, the words picked right out of my brain!

He said also, "The O'Hara dialogue sparkles."

He said, "Much of the music has charm, particularly, 'If Only,' 'Little White Nightie,' 'What I Want Is You,' 'Catch Colt.' "

He gave a complete and detailed description of the

whole play, the names of everyone in it, what parts they played, and how they played them, giving generous credit wherever it was deserved. Jimmie, particularly, got a whole paragraph praising the warmth and beauty of his voice, his excellent rendering of the part.

All the same, it was no rave. I knew he had reservations, and thought that probably he was not hopeful for the play's future. I wanted to know what his reservations were. We exchanged some notes, and at last he wrote me.

"If you really want to know, I think the play is all right. I don't see anything wrong with it. I don't mind the long talky scene between the cook and the boy which some people object to, because I think they did well with their parts. What I do feel is that the whole play lacks *dynamism*. I can only call it that. And that is just what musicals have—ought to have—the thing that puts them over."

I agreed. I was shaken, but it was exciting and challenging too. Dynamism!! What was it really? It was that speed, snap, push; that controlled but almost explosive violence that drives the scenes of a musical from beginning to end without pause or hesitation or wavering. As for instance, a great piano virtuoso would play a concert piece through, using every last cell of his body, and rise at the end to bow with his hair wringing wet, not a dry stitch of clothes on his body.

A Broadway producing company, successful and experienced, was certainly a virtuoso. But we were not. With what we had had to date, this could not have been expected. But the script? I wondered how much dynamism—or lack of it—was inherent in the script. Probably a good deal.

[250]

In my mind, I began to trim and tighten the script. Yes, again! I wound the tension tighter.

Many of my songs ended with a little postlude (while audience waited to clap and finally decided not to) and some began with a little prelude (while actors stood waiting to open their mouths and sing).

As night by night I sat watching the show, all my thought was on this. I lopped off beginnings and endings; brought scenes together quicker, tighter; did more with lights, less with visible on-stage movements; did away with all props not absolutely needed; reduced the number of sets and set changes to half. And so began to make the shape of the next, the third try-out.

This was the one that must be right.

As for what Kirk Knox had said, I took comfort from one thing.

By his own confession, he was not qualified to judge of the music. And whenever the play had aroused real enthusiasm it had been for the music.

There was one important engagement I had been looking forward to with pleasure. This was a luncheon given for me at the Plains Hotel on the Wednesday following opening night (which was on Monday) by the Women's Press Club of Wyoming.

I did not know it was going to be such a large affair.

All morning the buses rolled in from the four corners of Wyoming. The ballroom of the hotel was crowded with women and men of the press, standees at the back and in the corners. I stood on the dais with my interviewer and microphones and answered questions, not knowing that we were hooked up to London and

Paris. Yes, after all these years the friends in France and England who had been won by those simple stories about that little filly, Flicka, and the beautiful world she lived in, were still interested to hear the voice and opinions of the author.

Since the title of the show had been changed on opening night, I had evaded giving any reason for it, I was saving that for a discussion at this luncheon.

When it came at last: "Why did you change the title to *Top O' The Big Hill?*" I was ready for it. I wanted their opinions. I wanted, practically, to put it to the vote. I wanted Cheyenne to talk about it. (It did.) I wanted the newspapers to write about it. (They did.)

The dining room buzzed with discussion—and the concerted opinion emerged. *The Catch Colt.*

No one cared for *Top O' The Big Hill.* I did not myself. The moment I saw it over the theatre I knew it was a flop. Why? I don't know. Perhaps that "o' " instead of "of." Something cute and coy about it. Like "Hop o' my Thumb."

But *Catch Colt* was it.

When the *Tribune* came out next morning, it announced the decision.

This, I felt, must be reported to Jean Dalrymple. After the Washington show she had written me: ". . . I did not come down because I heard from some of my pals that the show had not quite jelled, and I knew you would not want me to see it until it had."

She had not come to the Cheyenne show either.

Now I sent her a copy of the *Tribune* reporting the luncheon and the discussion about the title. I marked the lines which linked the title of *The Catch Colt* with the final song of the show which has the same title: ". . . perhaps the most appealing music of all."

She wrote me immediately, acknowledging my letter and enclosure and saying ". . . this being the case, *The Catch Colt* is probably the right title after all."

So it was unanimous.

Thirty-One

I HAVE SAVED for the last the brief description of a sort of disaster that descended upon us from those rolling plains of the west, or rather that we thrust ourselves into as, at great expense, we drove, flew, chugged, or otherwise proceeded into them.

Cheyenne was not only the capital of Wyoming, it was also, ecclesiastically speaking, the capital of the Church in that state.

The Roman Catholic cathedral was one of the finest buildings in town.

That the Catholic University of America should bring a student group from Washington to Cheyenne and run a university-made production at the Lincoln Theatre was news for Catholics everywhere.

That they should do it during the week of "Frontier Days" left the heads of the Diocese wondering who was crazy. As a priest-reporter from the *Wyoming Catholic Register* explained to Dr. Paul, it was the one week in the year when the forces of Good struggled almost hopelessly with the forces of Evil. The famous Rodeo attracted the worst elements of the state, for general hell-raising as well as for the Rodeo. Did we expect them to provide audiences for a "folk tale of the western plains?" For an almost classical Musical Play? What use even to open the theatre? Why? . . . . and why? . . . why?

But the deed was already done. The town was placarded with announcements linking the two shows. And tickets (a few) were selling.

As it was much too late to stop the ball rolling, the reverend gentlemen put their heads together and decided on the general tenor of the newspaper announcement.

A NEW DIMENSION SOUGHT FOR FRONTIER WEEK.

We found that the reporter had exaggerated nothing.

It was a sort of saturnalia. The streets were filled with milling mobs which sent up an unremitting roar punctuated by the clanging bells and sirens of police wagons. Occasionally there was the sound of guns going off.

Against this Jimmie Gilleran was singing, "That little white nightie, so prissy, with tucking in front—very neat."

But that was not all.

When the Frontier Committee discovered, early in the week, that it was a poor season, that tickets to the big show were not selling well, they put on an evening show in addition to the afternoon. The announcements that blared forth every hour or so roared, "Come to our evening show at Frontier Park!" and said nothing about our Musical.

We were in competition!

Our audience melted.

But we now knew about that ingenious method of filling a theatre which we had not known about in time for our Washington first night.

Kent went out to the Air Force base at Fort Warren and had a talk with the people in charge of Recreational Services. They were delighted to have free tickets available for Post personnel.

At the theatre, just before opening time, the house began to fill with uniforms. We had an audience!

And how they applauded!

That last performance was memorable for another reason.

I had never recovered from my discontent with the big barn curtain, the barn with the blazing sunset above it. I told Bill that before we left Cheyenne I wanted to see what the stage would look like without it.

I was ready to hear him say "over my dead body" or words to that effect and he promptly did, so I explained, "I'm not thinking of it for tonight, of course, that would be impossible. But it's an experiment which will help me plan the next production."

In that case, said Bill, if I would go over with him fifteen minutes before the show opened, he could let me see what I wanted.

Well, I stood in that dark theatre, alone except for Bill standing behind me, while the stagehands removed that curtain, lit the stage and showed me the set with nothing but the green ground cover and that elevation at the base of the cyclorama which carried the green rolling turf off into illimitable miles of mysterious distance.

I was spellbound. It was too good to be true. So simple. So thrilling.

[256]

I heard the hesitant but always highly literate speech of my designer behind me: "I. . . . am. . . . not. . . . unalterably. . . . against it."

"Then we'll have it like that for tonight, Bill."

So this breath-taking glimpse of the rolling and undulating plains met the astonished gaze of Dr. Paul as he stood there on the podium and lifted his eyes from the score.

An audible breath, a murmur, ran through the house.

There was a miracle on our stage.

They say that an audience is an actual part of a show. A show played to empty seats cannot be the same as a show played to a full house.

Certainly the vibrations—all that quivering electricity in the air—are different. That night we had it. (I wish Kirk Knox had been present).

And I wish Matt had been present too for on this night "I Have a True Love," the song he tried to leave out of the show on the score of its being "operatic," did actually stop the show.

There was always vigorous applause for this number.

Dr. Paul and I had agreed that the applause must not be allowed to continue too long, since the next song, "Green Grass of Wyoming," followed immediately.

The applause broke out: a crash. It continued in a steady volume. Dr. Paul stood waiting, his back still to the audience. The violinists put their bows to the strings, ready to start the next song. The applause did not abate. Dr. Paul raised both arms for silence, stood so waiting. . . . waiting—but there was no diminution of sound. The show was stopped.

At last Dr. Paul gave the signal. The orchestra played. The chorus sang eight, sixteen, twenty-four measures, while the house still thundered its liking for that unquestionably cantabile and operatic song, "I Have a True Love."

The big moving van was waiting in the alley behind the theatre.

Before the last of the audience had left, the stagehands were disassembling the sets, taking down the curtains. Bill, Vincent, electricians, grips; the whole crew worked until dawn, until the last milking pail, the last cowboy boot or ten gallon hat, was packed and stored away and the van was rolling out of Cheyenne heading for my big barn at Tyrawley.

In a matter of hours our rooms at the Hitching Post were empty. The automobiles, carrying cast, orchestra, staff, were on the road. Kent and I were in a T.W.A. jet, floating eastward.

John Philibert, baritone-bass, understudy for the leading part which he had never got to play, had spent all his money, had found no place in anyone's car, and was standing at the edge of Route Thirty, his thumb pointing east. Only three thousand miles to go.

In Cheyenne, they were thinking it over and summing it up: a good show; except for the slow opening.

EPILOGUE

MAKING THE NEW shape of the play was not a matter of cutting out chunks but of contracting every part. As if all the pieces of a jigsaw puzzle were made smaller and yet the picture remains the same. Dialogue was cut to the minimum, comings and goings eliminated. The script was soon done; when the music was finished too, a year and a half had passed. The play was twenty minutes shorter.

There was one big change. The opening. I was able, now, to put back the locomotive I had so regretted taking out. Headlight, bell, throbbing engine on the dark stage. And when the engineer delivers his introductory monologue, all is told that needs to be; about the sheepherders, milkmaids, and Letty. There was time, too, for that *réprise* everyone wanted, the railroad chorus; also for the sound effect of the express train rushing past.

There were results of the Cheyenne show. Sam Fox Publishing Company looking for more sales for "Green Grass of Wyoming," offered us $50,000 if and when we might want to put the play into an off-Broadway theatre. There was a condition: the rewriting of the music by a Broadway "modern" composer.

Kent visited the play brokers again. Dramatists Play Service was still considering musicals, but only tentatively. Possibly some time in the future. He left the new script with them.

On June 25th, 1963, Dramatists Play Service wrote me ". . . pleased to say we consider *The Catch Colt* as a beginning for our musical list. It develops as a simple, uncomplicated tale, suitable for amateur production . . ."

Publication would be when script, piano-vocal, orchestrations, plots for costumes and props, completely synchronized, had been delivered to them.

This was done. Contracts were signed. A first edition of a thousand copies was published. Announcements and advertisements appeared in all the trade journals.

And so ends the chronicle of the beginnings and nine years of the life of this project.

There is still its future, of which it could be said that it is the same as it was in the beginning, a dream. Except for one thing: that crack in the wall.

No—two things. For, as a congratulatory message from a New York theatrical man put it, "You've got your foot in the door."

Foot in the door? A foot in a door is a wedge.

So—anything can happen.

The book and lyrics of The Catch Colt are published by Dramatists Play Service and can be obtained at their offices, 440 Park Avenue South, New York, N.Y. Telephone—Murray Hill 3-8960